THE MUSIC MINISTER'S MANUAL

Foreword by
REV. DR. TOM BRIGHT-DAVIS

THE
MUSIC
MINISTERS'
MANUAL

Revised and Expanded

Leslie Pobee

XULON PRESS

Xulon Press
2301 Lucien Way #415
Maitland, FL 32751
407.339.4217
www.xulonpress.com

Paperback ISBN-13: 978-1-6628-4204-7
Ebook ISBN-13: 978-1-6628-4341-9

Endorsements

The Music Ministers' manual is a great book in all aspects. Leslie has written it from a wealth of experience in the Gospel music ministry. It is indeed a great manual, a must-have and must-read for all music ministers, pastors, church leaders, and all who are called into the service of God.

**–Rev. Francis Intiful, Founder and General Overseer
Anointed Jewels Ministry International**

This is brilliant; I wish this manual was available some 20 years ago when I set off on this journey...This is a must-read for all musicians and congregation alike.

**–Augustine Owusu Kofi Dua Anto (KODA), C.E.O.,
Chief Musician, Sound Engineer,
Koded Studios International**

In a time when some churches are merely 'worshipping the worship,' Leslie Pobee's book is leading the Church back to the pulsating core of God's moves amid His people. A fresh sound is being released from heaven at this very hour. It is aimed at bringing the Church in all spiritual jurisdictions across the earth, to a point of deep dissatisfaction with the 'old wine skin' ways of doing things. There is for that reason a noticeable Divine agenda to everything that the author says in this book. I can testify that he is certainly God's chosen messenger; chosen to put clarity and definition to that sound.

–Rev. Dr. Alex Phiri, Founder
Spirit Works International
Sheffield, United Kingdom

For me, this book is a compact library for Christian Music Ministers in their quest for excellence in their area of calling. I recommend it for Music Ministers at all levels of growth. For the young musicians, the book provides a clear road map for the journey. For the old guys, it is a tool for reflection and provides fresh insight into some grey areas.

–Eugene Zuta, Singer, Songwriter, Accra, Ghana

A must-read for all music ministers, true worshippers, and Christian leaders. Leslie Pobee has done a wonderful job introducing the heart of God regarding the ministry of praise and worship across cultures and generations. The Music Minister's Manual is a great resource and will contribute to revitalizing true worship in the church.

–Rev. Dominic Sarsah, Lead Pastor,
ICGC Life Temple, Plainfield, IL, USA

Finally, we have this book as a gift of God by the hands of Leslie to redeem the church from the pervasive corruption of worship in our age. The clarity of thought and depth of revelations profiled in this book makes it more valuable than material for music ministers alone. This is a must-read for every Christian and especially Ministers of the Gospel because true worship is an integral part of our faith. Behold! Leslie, the Doctor of Worship, Hear ye him!!

–Rev. Dr. Solomon Nortey,
Christian Apologist & Chief Speaker
Firebrand Inspiration, Accra, Ghana

Having served as a worship leader and a music director for more than a decade, I have lost count of the number of books and online materials I have read to learn about the music ministry. But I can say with confidence that this book by Leslie Pobee stands out above the others. He has, through the inspiration and direction of the Holy Spirit, captured within these chapters, some sensitive and essential information needed to return to biblical worship; something that is gradually disappearing from our modern corporate gatherings and worship. This is a must-read for not just music ministers but every serious worshipper!

–Joseph Amarteifio, Singer, Songwriter,
Worship Leader, and Music director
ICGC Life Temple, Plainfield, USA

Dedication

Affectionately dedicated to all music ministers
who want to serve God in their generation.

Acknowledgment

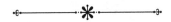

I am thankful to the men and women who have contributed to making this book a milestone.

Special thanks to Rev. Francis Intiful and Akua Assore Okyere-Siaw for editing this book. I want to thank my brother Ben Johnson for making valuable suggestions to this book. I also want to thank Winfred Whyte for taking up the challenge of designing this book and going back and forth with corrections, and not forgetting my brother Joshua Otsedzen for all his assistance. God richly bless you.

Special thanks go to my family, my dear wife Ruth for all her love and support throughout these years, and my beautiful children, Leslie Jr., Nathanael, Dorothy-Darling for being the best children one can ever ask for.

To all my friends whose love, loyalty, and respect inspire me to constantly walk in integrity.

God richly bless you!

Foreword

There is a revival gathering like large dark clouds preceding a heavy rainstorm. It is a revival that will cause men to have a new thirst and desire for God. This desire will burn in the hearts of men all over the world. It is a revival of true worship. Over the past 20 years or a little more, I have observed how God's hand is moving to prepare the whole of humanity for the unfolding of this grace and blessing. I have taken note that God is raising many like John the Baptist to cry out in the wilderness and desolate places to prepare many for this blessing. It is from this angle that I look at this book "The Music Minister's Manual" by our Brother Leslie Pobee. For anyone in the music ministry desiring to step up, be anointed, and use by God, this book will be an inspirational, revelational help, support, and source of information. Leslie's burden and passion are clear. He is simply saying that those who lead God's people in songs of the spirit and worship need to get their fundamentals right if they should do their tasks right. This book like many others for this time and season is a wake-up call to the church.

When Brother Leslie asked me to foreword this book, little did I know what I was getting myself into? I say this because I have a habit of properly scrutinizing books I am asked to foreword before doing so. I found this book extra packed and had to take quite a long time examining its issues. I must say, this is one of the most involving, thought-provoking, and bold writings I have come across in a long, long while. The attempt has been passionately made by Leslie to include everything a music minister should be concerned about if he wants to please God in everything, starting from his personal life. In this regard, Leslie's extensive research on the wide range of topics in this book cannot go without notice. He has given us a lot of "foods for thought."

The perspectives offered in this book, question our beliefs, church traditions, and convictions about the music ministry. To me, they are intended to provoke us to find God's perspective on what we consider grey areas when it comes to the Christian faith and music. He doesn't come across to me as one claiming to have all the answers or as one implying every opinion, he has expressed is perfect. Leslie simply gives you things to think about and consider through the eyes of the scriptures.

My expectation is that this book will help us all seek the truth about music and music ministry in the right direction and for all these, I am grateful to God for this book.

–Rev. Dr. Tom Bright-Davies, President, TBD Ministries
Chief Musician, Throneroom Family Choir
CEO, Piper's Music Consult, Accra, Ghana

Table of content

Introduction

The music ministry is one of the most important ministries in the church today. As an integral part of Christian worship and fellowship, the ministry carries a very strong unction and plays an important role in the tremendous work God is doing in these last days.

There is overwhelming evidence from church history that music played an active role in the different epochs of the church. During the beginnings of the Protestant, Pentecostal, and Charismatic Movements, music was very instrumental in the propagation of the Gospel. Music also featured prominently during the great reform that occurred in the nation of Israel under the leadership of King David.

The music ministry is one of the ministries, if not the only ministry, on earth today that will continue in eternity. The working of miracles, for example, will cease because God would have made all things perfect; His enemies would have become His foot stool (Psa. 110:1) and there will be no need for any supernatural intervention (Rev. 21:4-6). The preaching of the word of God would cease because the image of God would have been fully formed in us (1 Joh. 3:2) and we will be living with the Word. Even our faith will give way to sight (2 Cor. 5:7) and our hope will become experience (Rom. 8:24). According to John the Apostle, only love will remain because God is love (1 Joh. 4:8) and love is eternal. Since music helps us to better express our love to God, the sound of music will be heard throughout eternity (Rev. 5:9; Rev. 14:3) because we will be loving God throughout eternity.

Again, when we carefully examine all activities carried out during corporate worship, we will realize that the time of praise and worship is the only period, in the entire service that ministers directly to the Lord. All other activities are intended to meet the needs of the church. The time of intercession, for example, is used to intercede for the church, people in distress, and the lost world (1 Tim. 2:1). The sermon, on the other hand, exhorts, encourages, guides, comforts, rebukes, and molds the body into the image of Christ (2 Tim. 3:16-17). The announcements or notices also inform members of the church's impending programs and other meetings.

Music is an important part of our worship, although we can worship God and have meaningful fellowship with Him without it. As Murdock puts it, *"music conditions the heart to react and respond to the Holy Spirit."* [1] It does not enhance worship nor sustain our fellowship with God, it only creates the means of expressing our emotions that are founded on the truth of the Scriptures in worship. Miracles take place and revelations are received when the right atmosphere is created through music. Although music is the simplest medium to connect to God, it is not the easiest, as it requires a great deal of effort on our part. We need to allow the Holy Spirit to condition our

---

[1] (Murdock 1999)

hearts, using the truths of God's words in the songs we sing to bring us to that place where we can worship God acceptably.

Despite the role music plays in our relationship with God and in corporate worship, it is one of the ministries that is easily taken for granted by music ministers and church leaders alike. It is very easy for church leaders to admit individuals into the department, especially in startup/young churches because there may not be any structured way to recruit for the department. Again, because these young churches urgently need worship leaders, they allow just everyone to join the ministry. However, the fact that an individual can sing a few songs to make the congregation feel good or excited, does not mean everything is alright or that the individual is fit for the department. Members of the department need some training to bring them up to the standard that is in line with the mind of God for that local church as well as the church's vision and mission.

Other leaders believe that musicians should be able to produce good music whenever they are called upon. On the contrary, a lot of work goes into selecting songs; finding the key(s) that is good for the team, especially in cases where the musicians do not know the keys, learning the songs; and practicing them several times before they are sung at meetings. Another problem is that the time of praise and worship has become just one of the activities we do during Sundays and other Christian gatherings without any proper consideration. For some people, praise and worship is just an afterthought, simply because they have not understood the role music plays in our relationship with God.

I have also observed with great disappointment that whenever the church needs time for other activities on Sundays or other gatherings, it is the time allotted to praise and worship that is shortened to make room for those activities. Some teams are given as little as 10 minutes to minister, which in my opinion, is not enough to adequately praise the Lord. If that time is meant to prepare the atmosphere before the preacher ministers, then it is fine, but not to sing to God. In some instances, the time of praise is deliberately prolonged to buy time, while the congregation waits for a habitual *late-comer* preacher. We should not use the time meant for the Most-High God as "*a gap-filling activity.*"[2] The time of praise and worship should be treated as special because it is unto God.

The choir can sing a couple of songs while waiting for a guest preacher to minister because in my opinion, the choir ministers comfort, encouragement, and exhortation to the congregants but the praise and worship team ministers to God. Someone may ask, what if the church does not have a choir? The praise team can also play that role, however, the time that is known as "praise and worship" should be used to praise God and nothing else.

Again, some church leaders do not allocate adequate resources towards the development of the music department. So far as people are singing in church in the name of ministration, leaders turn to be ok with it. However, the fact that people are singing in the church may not be good enough for its growth. A lot more should be done to develop the department. Leadership needs to intentionally develop a long-term plan for the department, which may include training interested youth as musicians, sponsoring someone to take some causes in music, or even hiring a qualified musician to lead the team. Again,

---

[2] (Pobee 2009)

where there is no clear vision for the music department, the department does not grow. Proverbs 29:18 says *"Where there is no vision, the people perish..."* (NKJV). The music ministry is a direct reflection of the health of the church; when the church is thriving, it reflects in its music ministry and the reverse is also true. If you want your church to grow, invest in the music ministry – both in the people and musical instruments.

At times, leadership does not factor the department in the planning of the church's program. I am not just saying this from hearsay but experience. I have, in many instances, seen how the department has been deliberately disregarded in the planning of the church's programs, which has caused a lot of frustration for the praise leader/director, hampered the growth of the music department, and the local assembly. It is even worse in cases where the local pastor is a micro-manager; members of the department are moved in and out of the music department without considering how that may affect the department. Like any system, the ministry needs stability and very little interference to grow.

Individuals join the department without knowing the purpose of the ministry. They don't understand that their foremost duty is ministering to God rather than fulfilling their desires to be known or seen. No wonder those ministers use the department to show off their skills and attract attention to themselves rather than to God. This understanding comes from knowing God and spending time with Him. A lot of ministers do not wait to know the mind of God even before ministering, which is reflected in their ministration. Some music ministers do not know how to prepare their minds and heart, let alone, know how to select appropriate songs for service. They often select songs that neither praise nor worship the Lord and sing those songs during praise and worship.

Other challenges worship leaders face include properly arranging their songs for ministration, when to change their songs, how to introduce new songs during ministration, as well as how to carry themselves on stage. Consequently, they lose their sensitivity to the move of the Holy Spirit. Some worship leaders do not know what to do when the Spirit of God is moving, which song(s) the Spirit desires to move with, and when to be silent to allow the Spirit of God to speak to the congregation through word of wisdom, word of knowledge, or prophecy. These challenges make their ministration haphazard, lacking direction and focus. Sometimes ministers do not even know what to do after ministration and how to keep themselves until the next ministration.

Another challenge that often affects the department is uncommitted musicians. Uncommitted musicians are a canker to the growth of the department and ministry and their actions should not be tolerated. If they will not get committed to the ministry, it will be better for the department to function without them. They affect the quality of ministration and hinder the move of God. The work of the Holy Spirit is impeded when people are not fully yielded to the mandate of a particular local church. Remember, the Holy Spirit works in situations where people are willing and available.

When one examines the programs/curricula of Bible training institutions and seminaries, very little attention is placed on training ministers about the music ministry. Most Bible schools and colleges focus more on areas such as theology, Biblical Languages, Christian Apologetics, Christian Ministry, Divinity, just to name a few, but very little focus on the music ministry. All these subject areas are very important; however, I suggest that equal time be given to training preachers and other Christian professionals about the music ministry as it is a department young ministers will encounter in one way or another during their careers.

At the industry level, some artists no longer wait on God for inspiration and direction before recording new songs. Fame has become the focus of many gospel musicians instead of God. Some artists go on to record singles and even albums, solely based on their desire to remain on the scene. Sadly, those are the songs that make it to the charts, causing those artists to feel that they can do it without God. Some artists even pick secular songs, alter the melody, and change the lyrics to words that will appeal to the church and call them gospel music. There is a spirit behind every song that is released; it is either the Holy Spirit or something else. MacArthur stated that "*it is amazing how eager churches are today to adapt the music of the culture and try to sanitize it.*"[3] They forget that the spirit behind the melody, harmony, and lyrics of those songs they 'borrowed' does not change by just changing the lyrics. The music of the world is based on drugs, alcohol, and sex; the flesh. Why will the church want to be associated with it? This is just the scheme of the devil to rub the church off of the blessings that gospel songs bring.

With all these issues in mind, I offer this book as a tool to help address some of the concerns raised above and many more. It presents a holistic view of the music ministry as a way of guiding music ministers (vocalists and instrumentalists). I

---

[3] (MacArthur n.d.)

believe that this book will not just help music ministers adopt the best practices and avoid the pitfalls associated with the office, but it will also help pastors to implement measures that will build the music department and the local church. This book is also a direct follow-up to my maiden book: *"Thanksgiving and Praise: Believer's Assurance of Sustained Inflow of Divine Power"*, as it seeks to address some of the questions that came up after it.

I have divided the book into two parts: Part I provides detailed information about the music ministry and Part II provides some technical tips Music Ministers need to enhance their ministry. I have quoted extensively from the Bible to help you follow my lines of arguments and help you stay focused on the discussions in this book. I have also supported most of the points raised in this book with my own experiences and testimonies.

If you have any questions about the music ministry or the content of this book, please feel free to contact me at lesprutf@ gmail.com. You can also follow me on Instagram and Facebook, and Twitter @ Leslie Pobee, and YouTube @ Leslie Pobee Ministries.

Prayer

May the Lord anoint the content of this book so that it can bless and equip you to be an effective music minister, as well as make you a blessing to your generation, in Jesus' name, Amen!

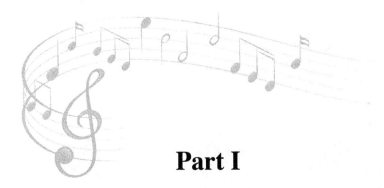

Part I

**Giving something of worth,
value, excellence, and merit to the Lord!**

Chapter 1

Worship, What is it?

O ne of the questions I struggled to find answers to in my early years as a music minister was the difference between praise and worship. I used to wonder whether praise was all about singing fast tempo or upbeat songs and worship, singing of slow-tempo songs. Well, that was the terminology I heard worship leaders use when I was growing up. I am very sure that the true meaning of worship still eludes a lot of Christians and music ministers, even today. Having the right knowledge will not only help ministers give their best to God in worship, but it will also help them know how to carry themselves as children of God. Knowing the true meaning of worship will help us stay focused and avoid the common mistakes most music ministers make.

Throughout church history, the definition of worship and the right way to worship have been very contentious. I dare to say that the definition of worship and by extension, liturgy, is foundational to the challenge of denominationalism the church has grappled with over the centuries, but that is a topic for another day. Worshipping God is very important, a desire that intensifies after the Holy Spirit convicts us of sin and brings us to the saving knowledge of Jesus Christ. I believe that God considers worship to be so important that He made it the first of the Ten Commandments He gave Moses. In the book of Deuteronomy, Moses instructs the people with these words: *"Be careful to obey all these regulations I am giving you ... be careful not to be ensnared by inquiring about their gods. You must not worship the LORD your God in their way. See that you do all I command you; do not add to it or take away from it"* (12:28-32). A better understanding of worship is critical in our relationship with the Lord.

I will start my discussion by examining the classical definition of worship, then to the Hebrew, Aramaic, and Greek definitions as used in the Bible. I will then examine some contemporary definitions of the subject before attempting to give my definition of worship based on all the definitions that I have outlined. At the end of the chapter, I will provide two examples of what I believe illustrates true worship: one from the Bible and the other from my life experience. Let's begin!

The word worship comes from the Anglo-Saxon word *'weorthscipe'*, which later developed into *'worthship'*, and then into *worship*.[4] This can be divided into two words: 'worth' and 'ship'. In other words, worship can be defined as giving (shipping/transporting) something of worth, value, excellence, and merit to the Lord. What can be more worthy, valuable, and excellent than a life redeemed by the blood of Christ that is willingly offered to the Lord? Webster's English dictionary defines 'to worship' as: "to adore or to pay homage." The

---

[4](Hughes 2006)

original languages of the Bible, i.e., Hebrew, Aramaic, and Greek, use different words to define worship. The Hebrew and Aramaic languages use three different words to describe worship, namely:

1. *"Atsab"* (Hebrew) means "to carve, that is, fabricate or fashion; to worry, pain or anger – displease, grieve, hurt, make, be sorry, vex, worship, wrest."5 This means that when you worry or get angry about every little thing, you are in a way worshipping because you do the bidding of someone. What do you worship when you are angry? Your guess is as good as mine! This word appears 17 times in the Old Testament but is mostly used in the Book of Jeremiah and relates to pagan worship.

   When you worry or get angry about every little thing, you are in a way worshipping because you do the bidding of someone.

   "And when we burned incense to the queen of heaven and poured out drink offerings unto her, did we make her cakes to worship (atsab) her, and pour out drink offerings unto her, without our men?" Jeremiah 44:19

2. *"Segid"* is another word translated as worship in the Bible. It is an Aramaic word and occurs 12 times in the book of Daniel. Segid means to "prostrate or worship"6 and it is used to refer to the worship of idols.

---

5 Strong 2009, #H6087)

6 (Strong 2009, # H5457)

> *"That at what time ye hear the sound of the cornet, flute, harp, sackbut, psaltery, dulcimer, and all kinds of musick, ye fall down and worship (segid) the golden image that Nebuchadnezzar the king hath set up."*
>
> *Daniel 3:5*

3. *"Shachah"* means to "prostrate, especially reflexively in homage to royalty or God; to bow oneself down, crouch, fall down flat, humbly beseech, do or make obeisance, do reverence".[7] This Hebrew word is used 193 times in the Old Testament, and it was first used when Abraham went to offer Isaac as a sacrifice to the Lord:

> *"And Abraham said unto his young men, Abide ye here with the ass; and I and the lad will go yonder and worship (shachah), and come again to you." Genesis 22:15*

> *"O come, let us worship (shachah) and bow down: let us kneel before the LORD our maker." Psalm 95:6*

It is clear from the above definitions that when it comes to worshipping Yahweh, *"Shachah"* was the worship the average Hebrew worshipper knew. To the Hebrews, this was the highest form of worship

Worship is illustrated as the action one takes towards God that is premised on the condition of the worshipper's heart.

---

[7] (Strong 2009, # H7812)

6

they could ever offer their Maker. It was the kind of worship they offered with all their heart, soul, and spirit (Mar. 12:30). In the two verses above, no references are made to verbalization or singing during worship; rather, worship is illustrated as the action one takes towards God that is premised on the condition of the worshipper's heart. In other words, true worship is not a physical or an outward act, but the state of the worshipper's heart, from the soulish realm, where only God, and in some cases, Satan, has access to. The aspect of our worship that becomes visible to people around us is our praise, which is the outworking of our worship.

The Greeks used six different words to define worship, which mainly revolved around the object of worship (see chapter 2). Below are the words and their meanings:

1. ***"Proskuneo"*** means "to kiss, like a dog licking his master's hand; to fawn or crouch to, that is, prostrate oneself in homage or do reverence to, adore".[8] *Proskuneo* occurs 60 times in the New Testament, and it relates to worshipping Yahweh. This was the form of worship the early believers practiced that earned them the name Christians (Act. 11:26); they simply loved the Lord and each other.

   "Saying, Where is he that is born King of the Jews? For we have seen his star in the east, and are come to worship (proskuneo) him."
   Matthew 2:2

[8] (Strong 2009, # H7812)

7

2. *"Sebomai"* means *"to revere, that is, adore: to be devout, religious, or to worship."*[9] It occurs 10 times in the New Testament and relates to worshipping God superficially.

> *"But in vain they do worship (Sebomai) me, teaching for doctrines the commandments of men".* **Matthew 15:9**

3. *"Doxa"* means "to dignify, glory, honor, praise or worship."[10] *Doxa* occurs 170 times in the New Testament and mostly relates to material splendor and glory.

> *"But when thou art bidden, go and sit down in the lowest room; that when he that bade thee cometh, he may say unto thee, Friend, go up higher: then shalt thou have worship (Doxa) in the presence of them that sit at meat with thee."* **Luke 14:10**

4. *"Latreuo"* means "to minister to God, that is, render religious homage." It also means to *"serve, do a service, or worship."*[11] The emphasis here is serving and it occurs 22 times out of which 3 is translated as worship and 15 times as serve.

> *"For we are the circumcision, which worship (latreuo) God in the spirit, and rejoice in*

---

[9] (Strong 2009, # G4576)

[10] (Strong 2009, # G1391)

[11] (Strong 2009, # G3000)

Christ Jesus, and have no confidence in the flesh." **Philippians 3:3**

5. *"Eusebeo"* means "to be pious towards God, or one's parents. It also means to respect, show piety or worship."[12] It occurs 3 times in the New Testament, and it applies to both God and humans.

> *"For as I passed by, and beheld your devotions, I found an altar with this inscription, TO THE UNKNOWN GOD. Whom, therefore, ye ignorantly worship (eusebeo), him declare I unto you".* **Acts 17:23**

6. *"Ethelothreskeia"* means "voluntary piety, that is, sanctimony-will worship."[13] It occurs two times in the New Testament and speaks of hypocritical worship.

> *"Which things have indeed a shew of wisdom in will worship (ethelothreskeia), and humility, and neglecting of the body; not in any honor to the satisfying of the flesh."* **Colossians 2:23**

I believe that the above definitions have given you some understanding of worship from the Greeks' perspective. When we have these definitions in mind while reading our Bible, studying, or ministering, we will apply them appropriately.

---

[12] (Strong 2009, # G2151)

[13] (Strong 2009, # G2152)

I now turn my focus to some contemporary definitions of worship. In his book titled: True Worship Experience, Rev. Eric Kwapong defined worship as "*a life of deep and abject submission, love and loyalty, dedication and absolute obedience to God.*"[14] Worship is about building a relationship in which you are completely sold out to the will of the Father. A Music Therapist, Lynda Tracy wrote: "*worship… is what we were created for: a relationship with God, in which we recognize and praise him for who he is, and he is worshipped as he desires to be worshipped.*" [15]

According to William Temple, the Archbishop of Canterbury: "*To worship is to quicken the conscience by the holiness of God, to feed the mind with the truth of God, to purge the imagination by the*

Engagement in worship meets our needs as human beings for purity, knowledge, beauty, love, and purpose.

beauty of God, to open the heart to the love of God, to devote the will to the purpose of God". [16] "*Engagement in worship meets our needs as human beings for purity, knowledge, beauty, love, and purpose.*" "*Music enables all of these to take place in us*", as cited by Tracy. [17]

According to the Garden City devotional 'Sounds of Judah: A musical Devotion on Praise', "*worship is the invisible act that takes place in the soul*", while "*our praise is a visible expression that can be seen.*"[18] That invincible act refers to the acts

---

[14] (Kwapong 2001)

[15] (Tracy 2005)

[16] (Tuttle 1989)

[17] (Tracy 2005)

[18] (GARDEN CITY 2021)

of honor, reverence, and approbation we offer the Lord that is based on the understanding of whom God is and honoring Him for what He's worth.

In John 4:23–24, Jesus said to the Samaritan woman:

"²³But the hour cometh, and now is, when the true worshippers shall worship the Father in spirit and in truth: for the Father seeketh such to worship him. ²⁴God is a Spirit: and they that worship him must worship him in spirit and in truth."

What do these verses mean? It is evident from this scripture that God is very interested in our worship. Worship must be offered in Spirit and in Truth. To worship the Father in Truth means to worship Him in the light of His word – the revelation you have received from the scriptures. It also means to worship the Lord in the sincerity of heart; to be honest about what you say, sing about, and do at every moment of your life. It reflects the state of your heart. If you say you adore the Lord, you should mean it. This was Jesus' issue with the Pharisees; they were not sincere in their devotion to God (Mar. 7:7-8). Worshipping the Father in Truth also means worshipping God the way Jesus taught us to. In His response to Thomas' question about showing him the way, Jesus called Himself the Truth: *"Jesus saith unto him, I am the way, the truth, and the life: no man cometh unto the Father, but by me"* (Joh. 14:6). This means that Jesus is the embodiment of true worship – a life of total surrender to the will of the Father.

> **"But unto every one of us is given grace according to the measure of the gift of Christ."**
> **Ephesians 4:7**

To worship the Father in Spirit, on the other hand, means to worship Him according to His will; according to the inner witness of His Spirit indwelling you. In other words, worshipping the Father in spirit means to worship God under the influence and direction of the Holy Spirit. This kind of worship is attained by developing a deeper relationship with the Lord. It stems from a knowing that cannot be explained or described; you just know it. This kind of worship is not casual, but it carries the highest form of reverence one can ever imagine; a type that is led by the Spirit of God and unique to the situation you find yourself in at different times. This type of worship is usually influenced by your life's experiences of who Jesus is to you; how He has revealed Himself – His character and ways – to you.

Paul in his epistle to the Romans says *"Therefore, I urge you, brothers and sisters, in view of God's mercy, to offer your bodies as a living sacrifice, holy and pleasing to God—this is your true and proper worship. Do not conform to the pattern of this world but be transformed by the renewing of your mind. Then you will be able to test and approve what God's will is— his good, pleasing and perfect will"* (12:1-2 NIV). These verses help us understand worship better because they give us a reason or motivation to worship God; *"in view of God's mercy."* By His mercy, God saved us by and through the finished work of Jesus Christ on the cross of Calvary. Understanding the enormity of the mercy we received is enough motivation for us to give ourselves to God in worship. Paul says in 2 Corinthians 5:21 that *"For he hath made him to be sin for us, who knew no sin; that we might be made the righteousness of God in him.* This is mercy; taking upon Himself our guilt and not giving us the punishment we deserve!

The manner of our worship is also summed up in the phrase *"to offer your bodies as a living sacrifice, holy and pleasing to God."* Offering our bodies is about giving the control of our lives – soul, spirit, and body – wholly to God, not as a sacrifice of dead works but living works. We cannot put our bodies on an altar to be burned, but we can relinquish control of our will to God. Paul told the Philippians to *"Let this mind be in you, which was also in Christ Jesus: Who, being in the form of God, thought it not robbery to be equal with God: But made himself of no reputation, and took upon him the form of a servant, and was made in the likeness of men: And being found in fashion as a man, he humbled himself, and became obedient unto death, even the death of the cross* (2:5-8). This is only possible *"by the renewing of your mind,"* which involves daily ridding our minds from the falsehoods and lies of this world and replacing them with the Truth of God's Word. Unless our minds are saturated with the Truth, our worship will not be pleasing to God. This is what Paul calls *"your true and proper worship."*

True worship is not an event but a life-long process. Life is supposed to be worship and worship life! MacArthur says that *"true worship is a permanent attitude because we worship in Christ Jesus and put no confidence in the flesh."*[19] In his book, The Purpose-Driven Life, Rick Warren wrote that *"worship is*

---

[19] (MacArthur n.d.)

not a part of your life; it is your life."[20] It is not about the style, volume, or tempo of the songs we sing during corporate worship. It is not even about the lyrics of the songs but the condition of our hearts. Paul told the Colossians that "*So whether you eat or drink or whatever you do, do it all for the glory of God*" (3:17). Martin Luther said, "*A dairymaid can milk cows to the glory of God*."[21] It is very possible to turn every activity into an act of worship by doing it to the "*praise, glory, and pleasure of God*."[22] When we say or sing: "I love you, Lord," is that what our heart is saying?

Rick Warren, in his book: The Purpose-Driven Life wrote that: "*worship is not for your benefit but for God's benefit*." He added that: "*When we worship, our goal is to bring pleasure to God, not ourselves*."[23] Revelation 4:11 says *"Thou art worthy, O Lord, to receive glory and honor and power: for thou hast created all things, and for thy pleasure, they are and were created."* The true worshipper will know that God desires that we help a brother or sister in need, relate to our family in a way that pleases the Lord; give of our time and resources for the work of God and for the welfare of others. In other words, worshipping God causes us to love God and treat people with the dignity and respect they deserve because we are all created in the image of God and that is just the way God wants them to be treated.

> *"[26]If any man among you seem to be religious (demonstrative in worship), and bridleth, not*

---

[20] (Warren 2002)

[21] (Rea 2021)

[22] (Warren 2002)

[23] (Warren 2002)

his tongue, but deceiveth his own heart, this man's religion is vain. ²⁷Pure religion and undefiled before God and the Father is this, to visit the fatherless and widows in their affliction, and to keep himself unspotted from the world." **James 1:26-27**

"And the King shall answer and say unto them, Verily I say unto you, Inasmuch as ye have done it unto one of the least of these my brethren, ye have done it unto me." **Matthew 25:40**

"Selling their possessions and goods, they gave to anyone as he had need." **Acts 2:45 NIV**

"¹⁶But to do good and to communicate forget not: for with such sacrifices God is well pleased. ¹⁷Obey them that have the rule over you and submit yourselves: for they watch for your souls, as they that must give account, that they may do it with joy, and not with grief: for that is unprofitable for you." **Hebrews 13:16-17**

Based on all the definitions we have looked at; it is evident that worship is a web of activities that are directly or indirectly connected to the way we use our lives to the glory of God. Any activity that falls short of pleasing or glorifying God is not the *"God-approved worship."* Hence, my definition of worship is: *"everything we do with our lives (soul, spirit, and body) that pleases God."* The emphasis is on the order – soul, spirit, and

THE MUSIC MINISTER'S MANUAL

body because I believe that this is the natural order of our worship. Our worship starts from the soul – the real you; the seat of reasoning, and actions and brings both the spirit and body in alignment and goes on to say to God "*I am at your service, Lord, just to do your bidding.*"

Worship is everything we do with our lives (soul, spirit, and body) that pleases God.

The Bible gives us a perfect illustration of true worship that encapsulates most of the Greek definitions mentioned in this book. It is the story of the sinful woman in the Gospel according to Luke.

> "*[36]And one of the Pharisees desired him that he would eat with him. And he went into the Pharisee's house and sat down to meat. [37]And, behold, a woman in the city, which was a sinner, when she knew that Jesus sat at meat in the Pharisee's house, brought an alabaster box of ointment, [38]And stood at his feet behind him weeping, and began to wash his feet with tears, and did wipe them with the hairs of her head, and kissed his feet, and anointed them with the ointment.*" **Luke 7:36-38**

In the passage, the woman is recorded to have gatecrashed Jesus' dinner in the house of one of the Pharisees. She was hungry for something more than food. She went into that house with a singular purpose, to offer her life to Him in worship, and every other thing had to wait until she was done. That reminds me of Jesus' interaction with the Samaritan woman at Jacob's

16

well that also touched on worship. The woman's request to Jesus was *"Sir, give me this water so that I won't get thirsty and have to keep coming here to draw water"* (Joh. 4:15). That was a request for something more satisfying than a material object. True worship is born out of a craving for something that only God can provide.

The passage records that this sinful woman stood at Jesus' feet weeping and washing his feet with tears. Although water may have been in limited supply in Jesus' time, I don't believe the woman could not have gotten a few cups of water to wash Jesus' feet from the house of the Pharisee if she wanted to. However, she wanted her worship to be authentic and unique; so, she decided to wash Jesus' feet with her teardrops. This woman then took her worship to a whole new level; she wiped the washed feet of Jesus with the hair of her head. Now stop right there! This is absolute insanity to a modern-day person. It would be ridiculous to ask a woman to wipe someone else's feet with her hair, even when our living conditions are better than it was in the days of Jesus, in terms of well-manicured lawns, pavements in our communities, our regular wearing of socks and shoes, which prevent our feet from getting dusty and dirty. But that was exactly what this woman chose as a towel to wipe Jesus' feet. Truth be told, women cherish and adore their hair and would spend a fortune to have their hair look gorgeous. However, to this woman, her hair was nothing but an object for her Master and Savior's use. This, in my opinion, is the greatest example of reverence – *Sebomai*.

This woman took this worship thing a notch higher; she kissed Jesus' feet. To kiss someone's feet, whether the person is standing, sitting, or reclining, the person performing the act, had to be on their knees, crouched, or prostrated – *Proskuneo*. Like David, this woman was telling Jesus that *"Because your love is better than life, my lips will glorify you"* (Psa. 63:3 NIV). This woman sealed her worship by anointing Jesus' feet with an expensive ointment; the box of alabaster ointment (*latreuo, Doxa*). The aroma of this ointment fill the entire room and everyone that went out of that room had the scent of the ointment on them. This tells us that true worship is infectious, you cannot participate in or witness true worship and not get 'infected'. Oh! What a worship? For the complete exposition on the story of this sinful woman, please get a copy of my book: *"Thanksgiving and Praise: Believers' Assurance of Sustained Inflow of Divine Power"*. [24] Every time I read this woman's story, I ask God to help me to worship Him like her.

Jesus' response to this woman's worship was very interesting. It was an indication that this is the kind of worship that pleases God; giving of your very self to honor and glorify God. Nothing moves God more than heartfelt worship.

> **[44]Then He turned to the woman and said to Simon, "Do you see this woman? I entered your house; you gave Me no water for My feet, but she has washed My feet with her tears and wiped them with the hair of her head. [45]You gave Me no kiss, but this woman has not ceased to kiss My feet since the time I came in. [46]You did not anoint My head with oil, but this woman has anointed My feet with fragrant oil. [47]Therefore I say to you, her sins, which are**

---

[24] (Pobee 2009)

many, are forgiven, for she loved much. But
to whom little is forgiven, the same loves little."
48Then He said to her, "Your sins are forgiven."
Luke 7:44-48

Let me tell you about my first encounter with a different kind of worshipper. I was a high schooler in the early 1990s in one of the prestigious boarding high schools in Ghana. There was a student-operated and managed Christian fellowship known as Scripture Union (SU). The fellowship had an executive council, which planned and ran all its programs. Although we had the supervision of some of our teachers, the student executive body did everything. It was a real learning opportunity for me. The fellowship was so popular in those days that it was the pride of the principals of high schools that had one. Principals boasted a lot about the impact the fellowship had on the moral uprightness of their students. Other principals who did not have Scripture Unions (SUs) in their high schools did all they could to have the fellowship established in their schools.

When my cohort started high school, we met the last two cohorts of the Advanced-level (A-level) students. At that time the governments of many West African countries, including Ghana, were transitioning from the British A-level high school system, which lasted for 7 years to the West African high school system that only ran for 3 years.

Our Scripture Union met on Sundays before lunch, and we had three other meetings at our house level during the week. It was a haven for me because I was going through a lot of trauma at that time. I quickly got committed to the SU when I joined and never missed any of the meetings until I completed high school. The SU secretary at the time was also the praise leader. This young man was a different kind of worshipper; a kind I have never seen before.

During our praise and worship time, this young man would sing, dance, lay and roll on the floor until his white long-sleeve shirt and khaki trousers (pants), which was our ceremonial/Sunday attire at that time, would turn reddish-brown from our dusty floor. I used to wonder why this young man would want to make himself so dirty in the name of praising God. I used to imagine how he would worship if he was to appear in person before God. It was not until years later that I understood that this young man may have had a personal revelation of who the Lord is. This young man simply loved the Lord. I don't think I have that level of revelation today. Will you be surprised if I told you that this young man is a pastor of a big church in the UK, I bet not?

Little did I know that just watching this young man worship the Lord from afar would have such a profound impact on my life. But I am thankful to God for bringing me into contact with this young man's style of worship because it helped shape my music ministry. I have gone on to be a worship leader, ministering in many countries on different continents, writing books on praise and worship, composing and recording many songs. Looking back today, I wonder why I did not get closer to this young man, I could have learned so much from him and I am sure he would have been willing to teach me a lot more. Well, I was just a Form one boy (Freshman) at the time.

Prayer

May the God who gives His people the grace to love Him ignite in you the desire to worship Him more than you have ever done, in Jesus' name, Amen!

In the next chapter, we will look at the pattern of worship, as it is done in heaven.

Chapter 2

Worship, as it is in Heaven

I believe that most of us, if not all of us, somewhere along our journey as Christians, have prayed *"Your will be done on earth as it is in heaven"* (Mat. 6:10 GW), yet it appears that we often do not see the

The condition prevailing in heaven that allows the will of God to be done there is often missing here on earth.

perfect will of God working out in our lives. We claim to stand on the scriptures, pray and lay claim to every promise of God but those promises do not always play out in our lives. This is because the condition prevailing in heaven that allows the will of God to be done there is often missing in our lives and on earth. What is the condition prevailing in heaven that causes God's will to be done there? Let's find out:

> *"¹I urge you, therefore, brothers, by the mercies of God, to offer your bodies as a living sacrifice, holy and pleasing to God, your spiritual worship. ²Do not conform yourselves to this*

> *age but be transformed by the renewal of your*
> *mind, that you may discern what is the will of*
> *God, what is good and pleasing and perfect."*
> **Romans 12:1-2 NAB**

The first condition mentioned by Paul is the offering of our lives to God in worship. The absence of an uninterrupted atmosphere of worship in our lives is the main factor hindering the perfect will of God from working out on earth. I am not only referring to the moments of worship we have during church services, our private devotions, and prayer time but our continual fellowship with God and one another.

Everyone likes to be in environments where they are loved and appreciated. Similarly, God likes to be around people who love and appreciate Him. God is a gentleman and does not force His will on anyone, so when we create an atmosphere suitable for habitation and fellowship, He will certainly show up. When that atmosphere is absent, His best is not done in our lives, even when we stand on His word and lay claim to all His promises, although that is His desire.

Often, the best we get from God is His goodwill, and sometimes, His acceptable will. However, His perfect will is mostly unattained because we do not create the atmosphere of worship that matches the atmosphere – reverence, honor, praise, and glory – created in heaven. God is, therefore, not working at full capacity among His children. We are saddled with the cares of this world to the extent that we make very little or no room at all for God in our daily lives.

In the Scripture above, Paul asks us to present our bodies as a living sacrifice (Rom. 12:1-2). But why? In Chapter 11 of his epistle to the Romans, He stated and justified the reason why God temporarily abandoned the people of Israel. Verse 17 says: *"You Gentiles are like branches of a wild olive tree that were made to be part of a cultivated olive tree. You have taken the place of some branches that were cut away from it. And because of this, you enjoy the blessings that come from being part of that cultivated tree"* (CEV). We were originally not part of God's family as a result of sin, however, through the death and resurrection of Christ, we have become part of the family of God. Paul is drawing our attention to the enormity of God's mercy to physically present our bodies to Him in worship and rationally respond to His truth as His loving kindness carries us away to a point of spiritual renewal.

Worship is the reason why we were created (Ecc. 12:13; Rev. 4:11). A. W. Tozer confirms this when he stated that *"worship is the normal employment of human beings."*[25] Sadly, for most of us, worship has been relegated to Sundays and other Christian gatherings. We make very little room for God; how then will His desire and purpose be done in our lives? We need to consciously make worship our lifestyle by intentionally cultivating it. Most of us spend so many years studying for degrees; yet we spend very little time perfecting the purpose for our existence – worship. Some of us have piled up degrees even more than the thermometer and yet know very little about God's approved worship.

Most of us spend so many years studying for degrees; yet, we spend very little time perfecting the purpose for our existence.

---

[25] (Tozer 2006)

Please do not misunderstand me, I am not against people pursuing a degree or career, I am only admonishing you to let your learning and career help you worship God better. If you end up as a medical doctor, treat and care for your patients to the glory and honor of God. If your studies eventually make you an accountant or a marketing officer, you should not use your knowledge to commit economic crimes or exploit your customers.

> *"¹⁶Let the word of Christ dwell in you richly in all wisdom; teaching and admonishing one another in psalms and hymns and spiritual songs, singing with grace in your hearts to the Lord. ¹⁷And whatsoever ye do in word or deed, do all in the name of the Lord Jesus, giving thanks to God and the Father by him."*
>
> **Colossians 3:16-17**

A lot of us Christians and music ministers are unable to worship God the way He desires because of the little knowledge and revelation we have about how God must be worshipped. Thankfully, the scriptures are replete with examples of how God ought to be worshipped. The book of Revelation provides profound insights as to how God is worshipped in heaven. But why should we be concerned about the kind of worship that takes place in heaven when we do not live there? We recall that Moses was instructed to erect a tent of worship in the wilderness according to the pattern that the Lord had shown him (Num. 8:4, Act. 7:44, and Heb. 8:5). Similarly, the standard of worship here on earth should follow the pattern of worship in heaven. This is our only sure guarantee that we will experience the perfect will of God on this earth.

In the remaining part of this chapter, I have used selected verses from the book of Revelation to give you a better understanding of how God is worshipped in heaven.

Worship, as it is in Heaven

"¹After these things I looked, and behold, a door standing open in heaven. And the first voice which I heard was like a trumpet speaking with me, saying, "Come up here, and I will show you things which must take place after this." ²Immediately I was in the Spirit, and behold, a throne set in heaven, and One sat on the throne. ³And He who sat there was like a jasper and a sardius stone in appearance; and there was a rainbow around the throne, in appearance like an emerald. ⁴Around the throne were twenty-four thrones, and on the thrones, I saw twenty-four elders sitting, clothed in white robes; and they had crowns of gold on their heads. ⁵And from the throne proceeded lightnings, thunderings, and voices. Seven lamps of fire were burning before the throne, which are the seven Spirits of God. ⁶Before the throne there was a sea of glass, like crystal. And in the midst of the throne, and around the throne, were four living creatures full of eyes in front and in back. ⁷The first living creature was like

a lion, the second living creature like a calf, the third living creature had a face like a man, and the fourth living creature was like a flying eagle. [8] The four living creatures, each having six wings, were full of eyes around and within. And they do not rest day or night, saying:

"Holy, holy, holy, Lord God Almighty, Who was and is and is to come!"

[9] Whenever the living creatures give glory and honor and thanks to Him who sits on the throne, who lives forever and ever, [10] the twenty-four elders fall down before Him who sits on the throne and worship Him who lives forever and ever, and cast their crowns before the throne, saying:

[11] "You are worthy, O Lord, To receive glory and honor and power; For You created all things, And by Your will they exist and were created."
Revelation 4:1-11 NKJV

We all need a personal revelation of who God is to worship Him properly, which will only be received if we regularly study the scriptures, pray, and have fellowship with the Holy Spirit. Unlike the angels and saints in glory who know and appreciate the greatness of God's power and

True worship was one of the many things that were stolen from us when we fell to the deception of Satan.

awesomeness of His glory, and can worship Him appropriately, those of us here on earth cannot fully fathom His greatness and power, as such, we are unable to accord Him the reverence and glory He deserves.

Every community on earth has a form of worship they have practiced for centuries, which is a piece of evidence that the Creator programmed the art of worship in us. However, true worship was one of the many things that were stolen from us when we fell to the deception of Satan. We need to re-learn the art of true worship that we lost. This can be likened to an adult who is undergoing therapy to enable him/her to walk again after a near-fatal accident that destroyed their motor skills. This does not mean that they do not know how to walk, it is just that the installed program was corrupted and needs to be worked on. Similarly, God programmed the art of worship in us, but we lost it to sin, hence we need to re-learn how to worship.

We need that opened door (Joh. 14:6) into the reality of worship, as seen by John the Apostle (Rev. 4:1). That door can only open if Christ is truly the Lord of our life. Just as Paul the apostle prayed for the church in Ephesus, my prayer is:

> *"[17]That the God of our Lord Jesus Christ, the Father of glory may give to you a spirit of wisdom and revelation in the full knowledge of Him, [18]the eyes of your mind having been enlightened, for you to know what is the hope of His calling, and what are the riches of the glory of His inheritance in the saints,[19]and what is the surpassing greatness of His power toward us, the ones believing according to the*

working of His mighty strength ²⁰which He worked in Christ in raising Him from the dead; yea, He seated Him at His right hand in the heavenlies." **Ephesians 1:17-20**

What did John see when he looked through the opened door? He saw: The Object of worship, the Setting of worship, and heard the Theme of worship. Finally, John saw who the Worshipers were and what their occupation was. Let us delve a little deeper into these ideas.

1. The Object of Heavenly Worship

The first reason why a lot of us are unable to worship God as we ought to is that we do not know whom we worship. We also do not understand who He is. This was the same issue Paul addressed in his submission to the people of Athens when they wanted to get a better understanding of the ideas about Jesus that he was talking about.

²² Then Paul stood in the midst of the Areopagus and said, "Men of Athens, I perceive that in all things you are very religious; ²³ for as I was passing through and considering the objects of your worship, I even found an altar with this inscription:

TO THE UNKNOWN GOD.

Therefore, the One whom you worship without knowing, Him I proclaim to you: ^{24} God, who made the world and everything in it, since He is Lord of heaven and earth, does not dwell in temples made with hands. ^{25} Nor is He worshiped with men's hands, as though He needed anything since He gives to all life, breath, and all things." **Acts 17:22-25**

Just as Paul stated, many of us *"are very religious"* (Act. 17:22b) and claim to be worshipping the Almighty God, but in reality, we worship Satan through man-made things. The majority of us worship

We need to have a clear definition of the object of our worship, by committing to know God personally.

God with our lips but our hearts are after other gods (Isa. 29:13); especially, materialism. We need to have a clear definition of the object of our worship, by committing to know God personally. This was one of the understandings I receive in my early days as a Christian, so I sought to know God personally. I can say that I know God a little better than I did in the past. The world has gradually removed God from the center of our lives, so if we do not develop a personal relationship with God, our worship will not matter to God.

There were so many things in heaven at that time, however, nothing attracted John's attention other than the Throne and the One who sat on it. *Elohim* is the Occupant of the heavenly throne. He is the only qualified person worshipped in heaven.

31

On the contrary, He is not the only person worshipped here on earth. There are so many gods competing for our attention. For the perfect will of God to be done here on earth as it is in heaven, we need to make Him the focus of our worship.

When John looked through the opened door, he realized that God was described as: *"Holy, Holy, Holy ..."* This speaks of His absolute purity and perfection. Some Bible scholars believe that holiness is mentioned three times for emphasis. Others believe that it refers to each person of the Trinity. Whatever it means, one thing is certain and that is *"there is none like Him"* (1 Sam. 2:2). He is the Creator and *'Sustainer'* of the universe. He is the only Wise God. He is: *"...the Lord God Almighty"*- the omnipotent God; the controller of everything. There is no measure to His power. He is the one and only true God and many more. If we see God in this light, our worship would be beautiful and glorious.

Finally, the Father is described as the God: *".... who was and is and is to come."* He is eternal and has neither beginning nor end. He is the God who created time and seasons (Gen. 1:14) but stepped out of time into eternity. He knows the times and seasons (Job 24:1) and has the power to alter events to His pleasure (Dan. 2:21). Isaiah 46:10 says: *"Declaring the end from the beginning and from ancient times the things that are not yet done, saying, My counsel shall stand, and I will do all my pleasure."* Oh what an awesome God we serve!

He is God all by Himself, His existence does not depend on anyone. No one voted him into power, and no one can vote Him out of power; He is limitless in power, knowledge, and wisdom. Paul in His epistle to Timothy wrote *"Now to the King eternal, immortal, invisible, to God who alone is wise, be honor and glory forever and ever. Amen!"* (1 Tim. 1:17 NKJV). David said in Psalm 145:3 *"Great is the Lord, and greatly to be praised, and His greatness is unsearchable* (NKJV).

When we understand God in this way, nothing will hinder us from worshipping Him the way we ought, and nothing will stop Him from dwelling among us. There is a 'knowing' of God that cannot be explained and that is what we need to seek and find!

2. The Theme of Heavenly Worship

According to dictionary.com, a theme is *"a subject of discourse, discussion, meditation, or composi-tion, a unifying or dominant idea, motif, etc."* In music, a theme is *"a principal melodic subject in a musical composition."* Placing this definition within the context of our discussion, the theme of heavenly worship is the main idea that flowed

Until we value our Lord and see Him as worthy of giving our lives over to Him, we will not truly yield to Him during our private worship, let alone during corporate worship.

through the worship that John saw, which beautifully connected all the other activities in heaven together.

The *"worthiness of God"* (Rev. 4:11) was the unifying subject of meditation and the composition of that particular worship that John experienced. The Greek word for worthy is *"Axios"* (Strong's #G514), which means: *"deserving, compa-rable or suitable of praise and due reward."* That is the secret of true worship; the ability to recognize the person who is worthy of our devotion, praise, and honor. Worship is all about Jesus, the lamb who was slain (Rev. 5:8-14).

Humans naturally make time for things they value, thus, if God is deserving of a person's time, he/she will spend a lot of time doing His will and pleasing Him. Again, we give towards things we cherish, if God is worthy of our resources, we will give Him our very best. Until we value our Lord and see Him as worthy of giving our lives over to Him, we will not truly yield to Him during our private worship, let alone during corporate worship.

What is the theme of our corporate worship? Mr./Ms. music minister, what theme runs through the songs you select for praise and worship? Do you just pick any song because you think it will be good for the day's service or do you allow the Holy Spirit to guide your song selection? Some suggested themes for your song selection could be "worthy, blessed, wonderful, holy, etc." We rarely hear or speak about the worthiness, the blessedness, or even the Holiness of God at our gatherings these days. We mostly spend our worship time singing or praying about our needs as a church or individuals. Are our gatherings about genuinely honoring God or about us? We should do all we can in our power to make the attributes of our Lord and Christ the theme of every gathering of the church.

3. The Setting of Heavenly Worship

The setting refers to the place an event occurs. It could also refer to the atmosphere or the environment created by the event. In John's vision, the setting of worship was heaven, it was a scene of corporate worship, of synergy, harmony, and oneness of purpose. This tells us we cannot worship God acceptably when we are divided. Secondly, the heavenly worship took place in the throne room of God, where His glory dwells. True worship always occurs in the presence of God. We cannot live in sin and think we can worship God acceptably. Thanksgiving and praise are the vehicles into the throne room of God (Heb. 4:16). Finally, the scenery of the heavenly worship John experienced was that of absolute awe, wonder, and beauty. These are important ingredients of worship.

Revelation 4:3 says *"The one who was sitting there sparkled like precious stones of jasper and carnelian. A rainbow that looked like an emerald surrounded the throne"* (CEV). Precious stones speak of the mammoth worth and beauty of God and beauty is of the essence in worship (Psa. 29:2). There should be beauty in the way we sing; our posture and body movement during worship and beauty in the way the instruments are played. The Father desires to be worshipped in beauty and splendor. Whenever we gather in corporate worship, we should have one voice and purpose, i.e., to give God the highest praise that earth can ever produce in the beauty of holiness.

The rainbow around the throne speaks of God's faithfulness. He is a covenant-keeping God (Gen. 9:13-17). His faithfulness transcends every human limitation. An understanding of God's faithfulness will influence the way we worship Him. It is also recorded that there were lightning, thunder, and voices proceeding from the throne. These speak of the power of God, His awe, and unapproachable presence (Exo. 16-19; 20:18), yet He has given the New Testament Believer the grace to stand in His presence in fellowship. Let us use this opportunity to worship Him in holiness.

The seven lamps of fire burning before the throne represent the seven Spirits of God (Rev. 4:5). The Bible gives us the names of the seven Spirits of the Lord, these are: "...*the spirit of the LORD ..., the spirit of wisdom and understanding, the spirit of counsel and might, the spirit of knowledge and of the fear of the LORD*" (Isa. 11:2, read Exo. 25:31-40 for further understanding). These Spirits dwell in the atmosphere of worship and these seven Spirits enable us to experience the manifestation of the Holy Spirit in His fullness.

Unlike the heavenly beings who worship in the presence of God, we worship progressively; we move from the general presence of God into His specific presence – the Kabod.

Before the throne is a sea of glass, like crystal (Rev. 4:6). This speaks of calmness. The sea is usually boisterous, and it represents the rebellious nature of humanity. The calm sea tells us that in worship, there is no place for the boisterous nature of humanity. All must be calm!

"But the LORD is in his holy temple: let all the earth keep silence before him."
Habakkuk 2:20

"Be silent, O all flesh, before the LORD: for he is raised up out of his holy habitation."
Zechariah 2:13

"Let all things be done decently and in order."
1 Corinthians 14:40

Unlike the heavenly beings who worship in the presence of God, we worship progressively; we move from the general presence of God into His specific presence – *the Kabod*. This means we need to put in some effort to get on the mount of God (Psa. 24:3-5). Christ has indeed made the way for us to access the presence of God with ease, however, to dwell on the mount of God requires some work (Heb. 4:14-16). We need to graduate from being just a child of God to the beloved of God and that requires constant fellowship.

4. The Worshippers and their Occupation

The people who worship are also important because they make worship possible. Their actions are meant to reflect their perception, value, and reverence of the object of their worship. In our passage under consideration, the worshippers are the beasts, the 24 elders, and the host of angels. The Greek word translated as a beast is "*zoon*", and it is defined as "*a living being or a brute animal*". [26] According to Thayers Greek English Lexicon Of The New Testament, the word translated as beasts is noun neuter, which describes nouns and adjectives in languages such as Latin or German belonging to a separate gender that is neither masculine nor feminine.

The four beasts were covered with eyes round about them. The first beast was like a lion, and the second like an ox, and the third had a face like a man, and the fourth was like an eagle in flight. This means that there are representations of every living thing (Psa. 150:6) in the worship of Elohim. Each of the four beasts also had six wings. These beasts have some resemblance with those in Isaiah 6:2-3 (the seraphim) but appear to be different from those seen in the vision of Ezekiel chapters 1-10.

---

[26] (Strong 2009, # G2226)

The second group of worshippers is the 24 elders. The Greek word for elder is *"presbuteros"* and it is translated as *"a senior; specifically, an Israelite Sanhedrist; members of the celestial council or Christian presbyter"*.[27] The Thayers Greek English Lexicon Of The New Testament adds that the word *"presbuteros"* can also be used to mean an *"elder, in terms of age, a forefather, or senior in terms of rank or office. Among Christians, it refers to those who presided over assemblies or churches."*[28] These 24 elders around the throne are members of the heavenly Sanhedrin or court. Others believe the elders represent the saints in glory, the crowns of gold on their heads are their rewards for their faithfulness to God, and their white raiment signifies their victory over sin. Whoever they are, they actively participated in worshipping God. No matter how high you rise in society, you still need to worship God because He is your creator and sustainer; you exist because of His benevolence.

As a result of my many travels, I have had the opportunity to minister in many churches, and I have noticed that a lot of pastors and elders do not fully participate in worship. The pastors would either be in their office in the name of waiting upon the Lord before they preach their sermons or be moving around to ensure that everything is going on well. In my opinion, that is not right. Mr./Madam pastor, empower your helps team to ensure that everything is going on well so you can participate in worship. Again, these 24 elders were those who took council with God but whenever it was time to worship, they laid down their crowns and bowed in worship to the Most-High God. Mr./

---

[27] (Strong 2009, # G4245)

[28] (Thayer 2017)

Mrs. Pastor/Reverend or whoever you are, please actively partake in praise and worship because that is what God wants you to do.

The third group of worshippers in heaven is the host of angels numbering "*ten thousand times ten thousand, and thousands of thousands*" (Rev. 5:11). When Jesus returns for his church, the worshippers in heaven will include people from "*every kindred, tongue, and nation*" (Rev. 7:9). John records that "*when those beasts give glory and honor and thanks to him that sat on the throne..., the four and twenty elders fall down before him that sat on the throne, and worship him that liveth forever and ever, and cast their crowns before the throne*" (Rev. 4:9-10). This is a picture of perfect worship, and the ultimate goal of God is to see His redeemed united with one voice for one purpose–to worship Him. Wow! All these angels worship God in heaven, so who are you to think that God will not have others if you decide not to give Him the worship that He deserves.

Finally, it is evident that worship is the main occupation in heaven; "*...they do not rest day and night...*" (Rev. 4:8). On the contrary, worship is not the main occupation on earth. We are preoccupied with making money, raising our children, pursuing our careers, etc., for that reason, we have very little time for worship. This is one of the reasons why the perfect will of God is not done on earth as it is in heaven. We need to make worship our main occupation. You may ask, how? By

> *Worship is not the main occupation on earth. We are preoccupied with making money, raising our children, pursuing our careers, etc., and have very little time in worship.*

turning every activity of ours into worship! A good resource on this topic is the life story of Brother Lawrence in the book "The Practice of the Presence of God with Maxims."

Prayer

May God engrave the content of this chapter on the tablets of your heart, so you will always have the picture of heavenly worship in your mind when you are worshipping the Lord, in Jesus' name, Amen.

We will now turn our discussion to what music is, to better understand its role in worship.

Chapter 3

Music: What is it?

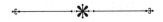

According to Webster's English Dictionary, music is "*any succession of sounds so modulated as to please the ear*." It is also defined as "*any combination of simultaneous sounds in accordance or harmony*". Music can be vocal or instrumental. "*Vocal music is the melody of a single voice or the harmony of two or more voices in concert. Instrumental music is produced by one or more instruments*".[29]

Music is one of the best ways of expressing our emotions. According to the International Standard Bible Encyclopedia (ISBE) music contains "*antitheses of joy and sorrow, hope and fear, faith and doubt, every shade and quality of sentiment can be found in music*."[30] For example, jazz causes people to feel cool; rock music thrust people into certain actions. Country and highlife (Ghanian folklore) music tell stories about life and relationships and finally, hip hop causes people to go wild. Music can ignite feelings of joy and sorrow, hope and fear,

---

[29] (Merriam-Webster 2011)

[30] (James et al. 1939)

faith, and doubt. This makes music a truly universal language of emotion.

Music was created to capture the minds and hearts of people, hence, we ought to select the songs we listen to with care because we are not of this world. Music is a gift of God to humanity. According to MacArthur *"it is a gift of God to allow believers to give expression of gratitude to God for who He is, what He's done, and particularly for our salvation."*[31] The International Standard Bible Encyclopedia (ISBE) states that any *"music that is used to interpret or accompany the Psalms is capable of expressing a great variety of moods and feelings."* [32] The lyrics of a song speak about the emotional state of the writer. What do you think about the emotional state of the author of the prose of the song: *"It is well with my soul"*? – Horatio Spafford [33] was *"passing through the valley of Baca"* (Psa. 84:6).

If music is just any combination of simultaneous sounds in accordance or harmony, what causes it to raise so much passion? There must be a force or spirit behind every piece of music, otherwise, it would not have the power to stir up so much emotion. It will not be wrong to say the lyrics, rhythm, melody, tempo, and harmony of every song are all influenced by a spirit, either the Spirit of God or the devil.

How can one determine whether a piece of music is godly or worldly? A succession of sound can only be called Christian or Gospel music if it contains portions of the word of God; inspires godliness and is pleasing to God's ears. Ken Puls has

---

[31] (MacArthur n.d.)

[32] (James et al. 1939)

[33] (Godtube 2021)

written a series of helpful questions that can be used to evaluate the doctrinal soundness of a piece of music we sing:

"Does it invite us into the presence of God? Does it focus our attention on God – His attributes and works? Does it call upon God to meet with us in worship? Does it declare and proclaim His Word to us? Does it help us confess our sin? Does it help us to rejoice in Christ and the forgiveness of sin? Does it teach us by expounding the truth of God's Word? Does it commission us to go out and live in obedience? Does it voice our prayers and petitions to God? Does it remind us of the promises of His Word? Does it express our praise and adoration to God? Does it express our thanksgiving to God? Does it voice our submission to God in obedience to His Word?"[34] Clayton Erb added that *"Are the words doctrinally sound? Is the text Biblical? Does it stimulate spiritual thought? Does it properly instruct? Does it inspire high spiritual ideals? Does the music fit the text? Does it fit the need? Does it produce a wholesome response? Do harmful associations come to mind when you remember the composer's name because of the musical style?* [35]

Any piece of music that cannot adequately answer any of the above questions is not Gospel music. When someone takes a worldly song and changes the lyrics but maintains the tempo, melody, and harmony, the person would have just dealt with one set of negative spirits leaving many others unattended to. So, it is not right to pick songs from worldly sources, change the lyrics, and think you have produced Christian/Gospel music (2 Cor. 6:14).

---

[34] (Puls 2007)

[35] (Erb 2009)

I remember watching an interview of a renowned jazz guitarist years ago. During the interview, the host asked his guest what his source of inspiration was. To my uttermost surprise, this musician mentioned Satan and that he was a member of the church of Satan. I was stunned; I just could not believe what I was hearing. That interview changed my perception of music. After that, I resolved never to listen to just any kind of music simply because it was appealing to my ears, or I felt good about it. It also made me serious about my relationship with God. I thought to myself that if Satan can give his followers such scintillating music, then my God can do better. As a music minister and a composer, I resolved to wait on God to give me fresh inspiration to write my songs. I also blocked my mind from every secular music. Since then, I can proudly say God has always given me new inspiration to write wonderful songs.

Finally, when we sing heartfelt songs to the Lord, it tells the Lord, we trust Him to do all that we need and ask of Him. The Lord also clothes Himself with the accolades contained in the song and acts upon them. When the songs we sing speak about the **P**erfection (**P**urity), **R**oyalty, **A**bundant Love, **I**ntegrity, **S**overeignty, and the **E**xcellence, that is, the **Praise** of Christ, [36] He arms Himself with the very attributes we sing about Him and performs wonders. Examine the lyrics of one of the songs the Lord gave me in 2008:

---

[36] (Pobee 2009)

King Jesus, we celebrate You
You are worthy of all our praise
Mighty conqueror
Great deliverer
You are worthy of all our praise

We celebrate You
O King of glory
We rejoice in Your victory
Precious Jesus
Reigning King
We celebrate Your royalty

King Jesus, we celebrate You
It's an honor to sing Your praise
Blessed Savior
You make all things new
We stand in awe of Your Holy name
©Leslie Pobee, 2008

Whenever a song like the one above – the God kind of song – is sung, it releases the spirit of worship that allows the Lord to wear the lyrics of the song and act in accordance. He becomes the Mighty conqueror and the Great deliverer the song says He is. He takes over the battles of our lives and brings victory. The Psalmist says: "*As your name is, O God, so is your praise to the ends of the earth…*" (Psa. 48:10). When we raise His song, the Lord steps in with unimaginable strength and becomes "*fearful in praises*" (Exo. 15:11).

> *"The LORD is my strength and song, and he
> has become my salvation: he is my God, and
> I will prepare him an habitation; my father's
> God, and I will exalt him."* **Exodus 15:2**

The habitation that Moses and the children of Israel were referring to in the above scripture is our hearts, which is also the target of the devil. Satan knows music is powerful and can capture the seat of our emotions, so he is working assiduously to conquer our airwaves as well as social media to control our minds. We should not permit him, otherwise, he will get the entire human race singing filthy and sensual songs, which will keep us out of the presence of God. The good news is that Satan is a loser who is fighting an already lost battle. The Apostle Peter in His second epistle says: *"His divine power has granted to us all things that pertain to life and godliness, through the knowledge of him who called us to his own glory and excellence"* (2 Pet 1:3)

We have all we need to overcome the devil! Sadly, secular music has also found its way into the church's repertoire. Mike Murdock in his book, The Young Minister's Handbook stated that: *"Satan is working hard at diluting the influence of music in our churches."*[37] He added that *"if music does not make me think about God or energize me toward God and His goals and dreams for my life, then it does not serve the purpose that God intended it to serve."* [38]

Do you know that God responds to the song of the redeemed? Music is one of the easiest means of getting the Lord's attention to our needs. When we pray, the Lord may send an angel

---

[37] (Murdock 1999)

[38] Ibid

to attend to our needs [39] (Rev. 8:3-4), however, when we praise Him, He inhabits our praises (Psa. 22:3). He says in Isaiah 42:8: *"...and My glory I will not give to another, nor my praise to carved images."* God will never send an angel to receive His praises; no angel in heaven can ever attempt to do so because that will be treason, especially in the light of what Lucifer did and the judgment that is awaiting him. Again, the Psalmist tells us that the Lord is holy, which means Christian songs must be holy, so God can find them suitable to inhabit.

> *"The LORD is my strength and song, and is become my salvation."* **Psalm 118:14**

> *"Behold, God is my salvation; I will trust, and not be afraid: for the LORD is my strength and my song; he also is become my salvation."* **Isaiah 12:2**

Where And When Did Music Start?

Music first took place in Heaven because God created it for His pleasure. However, the first evidence of music on earth, as recorded in the Bible, was in the city of Nod. The name Nod means: *"the land of wandering or vagrancy".*[40] This was the land Cain ran to after he was cursed by God for killing his brother Abel.

---

[39] (Baxter 2003)

[40] (Strong 2009, # H5113)

> *"And Cain went out from the presence of the LORD, and dwelt in the land of Nod, on the east of Eden." Genesis 4:16*

The man who started the music revolution on earth was Jubal, the son of Lamech, a descendent of Cain. He was a fifth-generation *Cainite*, the *"father of all such as handle the harp and organ"* (Gen. 4:21). The art and skill of making music were first discovered by a descendent of Cain. But why did the Lord give this important ministry to a descendent of a sinful man rather than to descendants of Seth?

> *"¹⁹And Lamech took unto him two wives: the name of the one was Adah and the name of the other Zillah. ²⁰And Adah bare Jabal: he was the father of such as dwell in tents, and of such as have cattle. ²¹And his brother's name was Jubal: he was the father of all such as handle the harp and organ." Genesis 4:19-21*

Two answers come to mind, the first probable answer is, since Jubal was the fifth generation *Cainite* and the number five speaks of grace,[41] it is likely that by the fifth generation the Lord had lifted the curse from the descendants of Cain who loved Him. Under the Old Covenant, the iniquities of the fathers were visited unto the third and fourth generation of children who hated the Lord (Exo. 20:5-6). It is likely that by the fifth generation, the knowledge of God had increased to the

---

[41] (McGawan 1997)

extent that Jubal joined the descendants of Seth to "*call upon the name of the Lord*" (Gen. 4:26).

By giving the gift to Jubal, the Lord teaches us He has the prerogative to show mercy upon whomever He wills. According to Mike Murdock, "*God created music to connect us to Him to energize us and accomplish His dreams for our lives*".[42] So, He gave the gift to the descendants of a sinful man to restore them to Himself.

> *"And he said, I will make all my goodness pass before thee, and I will proclaim the name of the LORD before thee; and will be gracious to whom I will be gracious, and will shew mercy on whom I will shew mercy."* **Exodus 33:19**

> *"Therefore hath he mercy on whom he will have mercy, and whom he will he hardeneth."*
> **Romans 9:18**

The second probable reason could be that when Lucifer fell from his heavenly office as the music and worship leader, God did not take the gift from him. In his quest to perpetuate his evil deeds, he gave the gift to the descendants of Cain, who then started the music revolution on earth. Can this explain why people who sing worldly or secular music are so talented?

The first answer is most likely because God is the giver of good gifts, (Jam. 1:17). Ephesians 4:8 also says "... *When he ascended up on high, he led captivity captive and gave gifts unto men.*" Satan has nothing good to offer but destruction. We

---

[42] (Murdock 1999)

are all witnesses to how the so-called renowned people, celebrities, and superstars end up as drug addicts, sexual perverts, or even commit suicide. "*The thief cometh not, but for to steal, and to kill, and to destroy: I am come that they might have life and that they might have it more abundantly*" (Joh. 10:10).

The Lord gave me a third reason why God gave this important gift to a Cainite. He said: "*I gave the musical gift to Jubal, the son of a sinful man because Jubal is a type of the church, and the descendants of Seth is a type of the nation of Israel. I did not give the gift to the descendants of Seth because I desired to raise another nation out of a sinful ancestry, the Gentiles, to be My vessels of praise. I decided to show Jubal mercy as a prelude to the grace I was going to make available to the world through My Son.*" Church, the Lord has given us this gift so we can use it to His glory. He has put a new song in our mouth and given us the mandate of making music, so let us rise and take our rightful place.

What Does the Name Jubal Mean?

According to Strong, the name Jubal means a stream. [43] The name comes from a primitive Hebrew root word "*yabal*", which means to "*flow; and to bring with pomp.*" It also means to "*bring forth, carry, and lead forth.*"[44] If the name means to flow and to bring forth with pomp, then it presupposes that the gift was given to Jubal by the Spirit of God, who was working in the 'shadows' (Heb. 10:1). According to Boschman in his book "*Rebirth of music*", the name Jubal has two meanings:

---

[43] (Strong 2009, # H3106)

[44] (Strong 2009, # H2986)

a fertile parcel of land and a stream of life.[45] These meanings speak of two attributes of the Holy Spirit (Joh. 7:38).

To be classified as a fertile parcel of land, the land ought to have all the nutrients needed to support different plants and animals. As the stream of life, it flows from this fertile land to the surrounding barren lands to make them fertile. The above meanings of the name Jubal support my earlier assertions that it was God who gave the gift of music to the descendants of Cain. It is of interest to know that out of the lineage of an evil man, the Lord could create such an enabling environment to give and support life. This land is so fertile that it can support any plant; no seed falls onto that soil and never germinates, grows, and bears fruits. On the other hand, no animal, whether carnivore or herbivore, starved or thirst when they were in the vicinity of Jubal. Just as God deposited the gift of music in Jubal, the Lord has deposited in every born-again musician the talent to make spirit-filled music that can bless His Body. Like Jubal, let us allow the Holy Spirit to flow through us and bring healing to the barrenness all around us.

Prayer

God, help us to use the privilege of being New Testament believers to produce and sing Spirit-filled music, in Jesus' name.

In the next chapter, I examine the role music plays in our worship. Some of the questions we will find answers to are: can we worship acceptably without music? What type of music should we sing in Church?

---

[45] (Boschman 1980)

Chapter 4

The Role of Music in Worship

The first two chapters on the meaning of worship made no direct references to the use of music in worship. Where then did the church get the idea of using music in worship? Can we worship God acceptably without using music? What is the role of music in our worship as Christians? Is music really important at all in worship? These are a few of the questions this chapter will answer.

As I mentioned earlier, historically, music held an important place in the social and religious life of the Israelites. The occasions and events during which music was used varied; however, worshipping Yahweh was the most important event or occasion during which music was used.[46] Since Christianity has its roots in Judaism, it implies the use of music in worship, as we have today, came from the early church. This claim cannot be detached from the fact that some aspects of Christian worship are influenced by the culture of the people practicing it. For example, the way music is played and sung during Christian

---

[46] (James et al. 1939)

gatherings in Asia is different from the way it is played and sung in Africa and America.

Under the Old Covenant, David was the one who incorporated music in corporate worship. As mentioned earlier, the use of music in worship was part of the great reform that took place in the nation of Israel under his rule. David separated the use of music in worship from the old order of worship that existed before his time. God loved this innovative way of worship and promised to rebuild the Tabernacle of David (Isa. 16:5; Amos 9:11; Act. 15:16). This speaks of the Church/the Body of Christ and explains why music is so important in Christian worship today. Music has become one of the important building blocks of the church. Again, singing together is one of the few things, including praying, that we can do together as the Body of Christ that makes sense and can help us stimulate each other to love Christ. As John MacArthur puts it, music *"is admittedly a powerful, emotional stimulator, it is a gift of God; a common grace."*[47]

The benefits of music in worship, both physically and spiritually, cannot be over-emphasized. Physically, studies have shown that *"various types of music can contribute to an increase or decrease in heart rate, respiration, blood pressure, muscle tension, muscle activity, and motor responses. Music affects peripheral skin temperature, gastric activity, and biochemical responses in the body. Involvement in learning music before the age of twelve contributes to increases in spatial intelligence and math skills. The implication of these facts about music, when connected with worship, is that those who are actively involved in the music of worship may be likely to*

---

[47] (MacArthur n.d.)

experience beneficial effects that extend outside the spiritual realm to improved physical and intellectual functioning."[48]

Spiritually, music has tremendous effects on the soul and minds of the hearer or singer. In 1 Samuel 16, Saul had a spirit tormenting him and his servant suggested that a musician be brought to play beautiful music to him to soothe his troubled soul, and also to drive away the evil spirit that was tormenting him. There are many examples in my life of how singing and playing music brought me relief from one worry or another. So, in the ensuing pages I have examined some specific roles music play in our everyday lives as Christians. The list may not be exhaustive, but it gives us great insights, which can guide our worship and, ultimately, our relationship with the Lord.

1. A Fundamental Part of the Church

Music is one of the pillars of the local church. These pillars: protocol, spirit-filled messages, and music, are strongly held together by prayer. Every local church needs the right code of conduct or ethics (modus operandi) to govern its activities. This is particularly important in the way the church relates to its members, the community, and visitors. The church's protocol may also spell out the duties of every member of the local church, its doctrinal stands, how grievances are resolved, etc.

Spirit-filled messages are important in building a strong and vibrant church and getting the members of the church in tune with God. A Spirit-filled message refers to inspirational messages offered in the right season; messages that reveal the mind

---

[48] (Tracy 2005)

of God for a particular time. Such messages come to meet the needs of the children of God at the right time (1 Chr. 12:32).

The final pillar of a local church is good music. As mentioned in the introduction, music played pivotal roles in the different epochs of the church's history. This is because music carries a very strong unction and can attract people to church every day. Apart from the role music played in the restoration of the worship of Yahweh under David, it was instrumental in spreading the Gospel of Christ during the Protestant Movement in the early 1900s, the Pentecostal, and the Charismatic Movements in the 1950s. For example, hymns played a crucial role in the great revivals under the Wesley Brothers, Evangelist Oral Roberts, Evangelist Jimmy Swaggart, and many others. It is certainly playing an important role in these last days.

The leadership of the local church should intentionally invest in musical instruments and other gadgets it needs, as well as in the skills of the people in the music department, if the church is serious about its growth.

For these reasons, the leadership of the local church should intentionally invest in musical instruments and other gadgets, as well as develop the skills of its musicians, if the church is serious about its growth. Leadership can also focus on training many of its young people to play an instrument or two if they are interested. This will ensure the growth of the department and the church. Parents of interested young people can even contribute towards their training. I know this might not work for a very small church, but as the saying goes "*where there is a will there is a way.*"

In situations where the church can hire a few instrumental-ists, it should do so. It will lighten the burden the absence of an instrumentalist places on the music minister who is supposed to concentrate on planning for service and praying for the team members. The absence of instrumentalists can be very tasking on the mind and spirit of the music minister. Sadly, an ailing music department is easily noticed by even the first-time vis-itor, as such, leadership should do all they can to have good music during every service. Remember, good music acts like a magnet that attracts people to church, similarly, poor music drives people away.

2. A Way of Expressing our Love for the Lord

In making music to the Lord, we express the noblest, deepest, and most worthy feelings of our hearts to Him. According to the Treasury of David, *"our triune God deserves the warmest love of all our hearts,"* [49] and music offers the right opportu-nity for believers to respond to the love of God. When music is used in the most desired form, those listening and experiencing it resonate with the beauty and move towards the same whole-ness, awareness, and harmony the music carries. MacArthur stated that *"music can be high, noble, and exalted. It can be elevating, uplifting, and it can raise that which is honorable and pure. It can literally tamper with all the ranges of human experience and emotion."*[50]

---

[49] (Spurgeon 1885)

[50] (MacArthur n.d.)

> *"Is anyone among you suffering? Let him pray.*
> *Is anyone cheerful? Let him sing praises."*
>
> **James 5:13 NASB**

> **[18]And do not be drunk with wine, in which is dis-**
> **sipation; but be filled with the Spirit, [19]speaking**
> **to one another in psalms and hymns and spiri-**
> **tual songs, singing and making melody in your**
> **heart to the Lord, [20]giving thanks always for**
> **all things to God the Father in the name of our**
> **Lord Jesus Christ, [21]submitting to one another**
> **in the fear of God. Ephesians 5:18-22 NKJV**

When we are filled with the Holy Spirit, as stated in Ephesians 5:18, we yield up everything of our own to allow the Spirit of God to control us, as such, we are able to sing to the Lord and "*speak to one another in psalms, hymns, and spiritual songs*" (v:19). Tracy wrote that "*the purpose of the music of biblical worship is to enable the worshiper to encounter the living God. The musical experiences of worship can communicate both verbal and nonverbal messages to the worshiper.*"[51] According to Leonard, music "*speak directly to the intuitive capacities ...bearing a sense of majesty, wonder, mystery, and delight, and brings a release of the soul even without recourse to words.*"[52]

Music is therefore one of the principal mediums through which Christians express our emotions in response to the truth of the Scriptures in worship. Through music, we allow the Holy

---

[51] (Tracy 2005)

[52] (Leonard 1993)

Spirit to condition our hearts, using the truths of God's words in the songs we sing to bring us to that place where we can worship God acceptably. It is also a catalyst of true worship and a 'vehicle' of our fellowship with God. The Psalmist wrote: *"And I will offer in His tent sacrifices with shouts of joy; I will sing, yes, I will sing praises to the Lord"* (Psa. 27:6 NASB). The Psalmist also added that: *"Praise Him with trumpet sound; praise Him with harp and lyre. Praise Him with timbrel and dancing; praise Him with stringed instruments and pipe"* (Psa. 150:3-4 NASB). Music is important in worship, however, God can be worshiped acceptably without music.

3. A Medium of Instructing, Teaching, Learning, and Propagating the Word of God

Apart from sermons, exhortations, and Bible studies, music is one of the mediums through which Christians get instructions in the word of God. The Psalmist says *"Thou art my hiding place; thou shalt preserve me from trouble; thou shalt compass me about with songs of deliverance. Selah. I will instruct thee and teach thee in the way which thou shalt go: I will guide thee with mine eye"* (Psa. 32:7-8). As we allow the Holy Spirit to fill us and envelop us in the Scriptures, the Christo-centric song we sing instructs us in the ways of God. Through Gospel music, Christians are instructed by God. When a piece of music is inspired by the Holy Spirit and its lyrics are taken from the Holy Scriptures, they serve the same purposes as sermons and exhortations.

> *"¹⁶All scripture is given by inspiration of God, and is profitable for doctrine, for reproof, for correction, for instruction in righteousness: ¹⁷That the man of God may be perfect, thoroughly furnished unto all good works."*
>
> *2 Timothy 3:16-17*

Music is also a means of propagating the Gospel, an outreach to the unsaved. Since the beginning of the church age, music has featured prominently in the different movements that have taken place in the Body of Christ. Musical concerts are used to minister the word of God to the unsaved. Scripture-inspired music convicts sinners. I have seen people running to God through the ministration of songs; it is powerful, and it works.

> *"So shall My Word be which goes forth from My mouth; it shall not return to Me empty, without accomplishing what I desire, and without succeeding in the matter for which I sent it."* **Isaiah 55:11**

Music is also a powerful way of teaching and learning about the word of God. Most of the Bible verses I learned as a child that I still remember are those that I was taught through songs. There is no substitute for a Spirit-filled song. Every Spirit-inspired piece of music teaches us some basic truths about the character and personality of God; about His plans for us as individuals and for the world. Music also affirms God's word and brings it to life.

The Psalmist says *"7...thou shalt compass me about with songs of deliverance. 8 I will instruct thee and teach thee in the way which thou shalt go: I will guide thee with mine eye"* (32:7-8). In other words, as we allow the songs of God to fill our hearts and minds, as well as instruct and teach us in the ways of God, they will deliver us from the trappings of this world that endanger our lives here on earth and rub us of the eternal bliss God has in store for us.

4. A Medium of Attracting God's Attention

Through music, we can draw the Lord's attention to our needs. Although it may appear easy, it is not the simplest medium through which we get God's attention. There was a time in their history when Israel launched a military campaign against Moab for refusing to pay tribute to them. Jehoram the son of Ahab, who was the king at that time, allied with Jehoshaphat, king of Judah and king of Edom to fight Moab. However, in the process, the troops ran out of drinking water, which meant they could become weak and not be able to fight their enemies. Upon realizing that the campaign was not turning out as planned, Jehoshaphat requested that they find a prophet who could tell them the mind of the Lord in that situation. Eventually, they were directed to Elisha the prophet, who told them what to do.

> *"12And Jehoshaphat said, The word of the LORD is with him. So the king of Israel and Jehoshaphat and the king of Edom went down to him. 13And Elisha said unto the king of*

> *Israel, What have I to do with thee? get thee*
> *to the prophets of thy father, and the prophets*
> *of thy mother. And the king of Israel said unto*
> *him, Nay: for the LORD hath called these three*
> *kings together, to deliver them into the hand of*
> *Moab. ¹⁴And Elisha said, As the LORD of hosts*
> *liveth, before whom I stand, surely, were it not*
> *that I regard the presence of Jehoshaphat the*
> *king of Judah, I would not look toward thee,*
> *nor see thee. ¹⁵But now bring me a minstrel.*
> *And it came to pass, when the minstrel played,*
> *that the hand of the LORD came upon him.*
> *¹⁶And he said, Thus saith the LORD, Make this*
> *valley full of ditches."* **2 Kings 3:12-16**

Elisha the prophet, did not have a word for them, so requested that a minstrel be brought to play skillfully before the Lord. Why did Elisha not ask for a prayer warrior but a musician? Elisha knew that at that particular time, music was the easiest way he would receive a message from the Lord for them. When the minstrel played the instrument, the hand of the Lord came upon him, and he instructed them as to what to do. I have personally found music to be a great source of direction in times of difficulty.

5. A Means of Exhorting, Encouraging and Comforting the Body of Christ

Apart from ministering to God, music edifies, encourages, and comforts the body of Christ. Colossians 3:16 says *"Let the word of Christ dwell in you richly in all wisdom; teaching and admonishing one another in psalms and hymns and spiritual songs, singing with grace in your hearts to the Lord."* When we allow the Spirit of God to fill our hearts, we make Spirit-filled songs, which God uses to teach and admonish us His ways.

Over the years, I have discovered that the songs that minister powerfully to me are those songs that were taken from the scriptures. Interestingly, those are the songs that always come to mind when I am in difficult situations, and I want to know the right decision to take.

What Kind of Music Should We Sing in Church?

Music was categorized into religious, secular, and instrumental pieces during the Renaissance period. The religious category includes Christian or Gospel Music. However, not all music sung in the church today is Christian/Gospel songs. What then makes a piece of music Gospel music? Does every song or music that has the name God or Jesus qualify to be classified as Gospel music? What is the place of instrumental pieces that have no lyrics? Since music has the power to arouse emotions and draw us closer to the Lord, or away from Him, we need to be circumspect in our choice of music.

According to Smith's Bible Dictionary, the word Gospel comes from the Anglo-Saxon word *"good message or good news."* It is of Greek origin–*"euaggelion,"* which literally means *"God spells or the story concerning God."* [53] The Gospel proclaims the love of God expressed through His forgiveness

---

[53] (Smith 2016)

and restoration of humanity to *'sonship'* through the finished work of Christ on the Cross of Calvary (Joh. 3:16).

A piece of music becomes Gospel music when it is Christ-centered, i.e., if it expresses aspects of God's love for humanity through the message and life of Christ. Every song or piece of music that does not have this message within its lyrics cannot be termed as Gospel music. Secondly, Gospel music should be inspired and backed by the Holy Spirit. When you have the Spirit of God living in your heart, you will easily tell whether a song is Spirit-filled or not; you just know it! Finally, the piece of music should inspire listeners to yearn for God and lead them to a life of holiness.

An instrumental piece of music, on the other hand, can only be classified as Gospel music if the composer is born again. James 3:12 says "*a fig tree cannot bear olive berries, either can a vine bear figs. A fountain can also not yield both salty and freshwater.*" Every born-again, Spirit-filled believer will only write, sing, and easily know when a piece of music is inspired by the Holy Spirit or not, because the Holy Spirit will bear witness of it in their hearts.

Music is an integral part of human existence, however, what is most important is the kind of music you listen to. The Psalmist says: "*He put a new song in my mouth, a song of praise to our God; many will see and fear and will trust in the Lord*" (Psa. 40:3). The kind of song you allow into your spirit can either shield or open you up to the devil's influence. What kind of song did the Lord put in the Psalmist's mouth? The piece of music or song was the God kind-of-song (Psa. 96:1), it was "*a song of praise to our God*", the song inspires "*the spirit of the fear of the Lord*" (Isa. 11:2), the song captures the heart of the hearers, and the song induces trust in the Lord. When a song is the Godkind of song, the Lord takes hold of the lyrics and rides upon it into every heart that hears it. This kind of song permeates every spiritual boundary. It sends the message of God to the perishing world and convicts them of sin unto repentance.

The Bible records that Jesus and His Disciples *"...sung a hymn, when they went out into the Mount of Olives."* (Mat. 26:30; Mar. 14:26). Evidence from the early church also alludes to the fact that music was an integral part of the church's growth. In Acts 2:46-47, we are told that the apostles and the new converts continued *"daily with one accord in the temple, and breaking bread from house to house, did eat their meat with gladness and singleness of heart, Praising God, and having favor with all the people. And the Lord added to the church daily such as should be saved."*

> *"Speaking to yourselves in psalms and hymns and spiritual songs, singing and making melody in your heart to the Lord."* **Ephesians 5:19**

> *"Let the word of Christ dwell in you richly in all wisdom; teaching and admonishing one another in psalms and hymns and spiritual songs, singing with grace in your hearts to the Lord."* **Colossians 3:16**

Through Paul's letters to the Ephesians and the Colossians, we are told the kind of songs we ought to sing during individual and corporate worship: *"psalms, hymns, and spiritual songs*," as we speak to one another through these songs and make melody in our hearts to the Lord. Singing is not an accessory to our worship or a filler in our service, but an essential part of our life with Christ. The apostle James also raised a similar point in his epistle to the church in Jerusalem. He wrote: "*Is any among you afflicted? Let him pray. Is any merry? let him sing psalms*" (Jam. 5:13). The Psalmist also commented about singing psalms to the Lord, when he wrote: "*Sing unto him, sing psalms unto him: talk ye of all his wondrous works*" (Psa. 105:2). The above scriptures state clearly that the most acceptable types of music to be used in worship are psalms, hymns, and spiritual songs. What makes this music unique? Let us examine these categories of songs closely.

1. Psalms

According to Hayford's commentary on Paul's Epistle to the Ephesians, "*psalms are songs whose lyrics are drawn directly from the Holy Scriptures.*" [54] In other words, the lyrics of the song are Bible verses. They are the words of God poetically arranged into musical scores. Since Psalms are the words of God, they are backed by the Spirit of God (Jer. 1:12) and can be used by the music minister to move the hand of God into action (Isa. 45:11).

> "*Sing unto him, sing psalms unto him: talk ye of all his wondrous works.*" *Psalm 105:2*

---

[54] (Hayford and Matsdorf 1991)

There are two Hebrew words from which the word psalm is translated, "*mizmor and zimrah*"[55], respectively. The former means "*instrumental music; by implication, a poem set to notes*," and the latter simply means "*a musical piece*." The Greek word for Psalm is "*Psalmos*" and it is translated to mean "*a set piece of music, that is, a sacred ode, accompanied with the voice, harp or other instruments*." [56]

Psalms are usually sung joyfully (Psa. 95:2) and are declarative[57] especially when they speak about the wondrous works of God (1 Chr. 16:9) and His greatness (Psa. 96:4; Psa. 145:3). They are usually accompanied by loud instruments. Psalms are "*Christo-centric*" because they adore, magnify and glorify Christ. James in his epistle recommended the singing of psalms by merrymakers; those rejoicing over the Lord's blessings. According to Gregory of Nyssa, a 4th Century writer, psalms are meant to be sung during "*the public worship of the church*", [58] however, one can also sing psalms during one's private worship.

> "*Is any among you afflicted? Let him pray. Is any merry? Let him sing psalms.*" **James 5:13**

> "*And let them sacrifice the sacrifices of thanksgiving, and declare his works with rejoicing.*"
> **Psalm 107:22**

---

[55] (Strong 2009, # H4210 and # H2172)

[56] (Strong 2009, # G5568)

[57] (Pobee 2009)

[58] (James et al. 1939)

Scholars believe the Psalms that carry the title *"Songs of Degrees or Ascents"* (Psa. 120 to 134) were sung during the sacred marches by worshippers as they journeyed to the great and holy feasts in Jerusalem (ISBE).[59] There were three festivals during which pilgrims gathered in Jerusalem to give thanks to God. [60] A contemporary example of a Psalm is a song sung by Don Moen entitled *"Trust in the Lord"* (Pro. 3:5).

2. Hymns

Hymns are *"humanly inspired lyrics in songs"*.[61] According to Webster's English dictionary *"A hymn among Christians is a short poem, composed for religious service, or a song of joy and praise to God. The word primarily expresses the tune, but it is used for the ode or poem."* [62] The Peoples New Testament says that hymns are *"songs which express spiritual emotions."*[63] Gregory of Nyssa wrote: *"hymns were mainly vocal song or ode. Hymns were the production, more or less spontaneous, of the individual member and usually not accompanied by instruments."* [64]

Hymns are born out of the writer's personal life's experience, such as trials, challenges, miracles, faith, etc. Hymns are also sung in direct praise to God. They encourage and strengthen our faith. This is the category of most contemporary Christian

---

[59] (James et al. 1939)

[60] (Brickner 2006)

[61] (Hayford and Matsdorf 1991)

[62] (Merriam-Webster 2011)

[63] (Johnson 2017)

[64] (James et al. 1939)

music. Hymns might not necessarily mention the name of God or Christ but are uplifting and motivational. According to the ISBE, [65] Luke chapters 1 and 2 contain hymns of Mary, Zacharias, and Simeon.

> *"And when they had sung a hymn, they went out into the Mount of Olives."* **Matthew 26:30**

3. Spiritual Songs

Spiritual songs are instantaneous rhythmic lyrics given by the Holy Spirit,[66] either in tongues or in an understandable language (1 Cor. 14:15). Spiritual songs occur when one is deeply connected to God through worship and prayer. Spiritual Songs are birthed after you have progressively moved from your spiritual outer court (where there are distractions, doubts, and fear) to the Holy of Holies (where there is love, peace, and joy) and the Spirit of God is groaning through you.

Singing spiritual songs is a New Testament phenomenon. There is no record in the Old Testament that refers to singing spiritual songs under the Old Covenant. The singing of spiritual songs came with the outpouring of the Holy Spirit, and it is the kind of music that is only associated with the church. This tells us how blessed we are to be partakers of this wonderful gift of the Holy Spirit. God desires to see and hear all His children, particularly, music ministers, worship Him in songs in the language of the Spirit. I do not know about you, but I am

---

[65] (James et al. 1939)

[66] (Hayford and Matsdorf 1991)

determined to use it whenever the Spirit of the Lord gives me utterance.

All through this chapter, we have discovered that music is an integral part of our existence and as Christians, we need to carefully choose the songs we sing or listen to. What song do you listen to or sing? Let us fill our hearts and minds with the Godkind of songs so that the earth will be filled with God's glory (Hab. 2:14).

Prayer

Father help us to fill our hearts and minds with the God kind of song so that through us the whole earth will be filled with Your glory, amen!

In the next chapter, we will turn our attention to the office of the music minister and examine it in more detail.

Chapter 5

The Office of a Music Minister

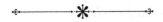

I n this chapter, I have examined the office of the music minister and the qualities music ministers should have. As already mentioned, the primary duty of the music minister is to use music to create the right atmosphere for God to meet His people in fellowship (2 Cor.6:4). We create this atmosphere by first and foremost ministering to God and then leading the people to also minister to Him. In other words, no minister can lead others into the presence of God if they have not been in the presence of God themselves. As we spent time in our closets feeding on His words, thanking, praising, and worshipping the Lord, we develop the skills and knowledge to lead others to do the same. In addition, worship leaders edify, encourage, and comfort the children of God (Rom. 14:19; 1 Cor. 10:23, 14:3; Eph. 4:29; Col. 4:6). We shall discuss this in much more detail in chapter six.

The term *'Music Minister*,' as used here, refers to both instrumentalists and vocalists. It includes those who offer direct praise to God (praise ministers. worship leaders, or praise leaders), those who play instruments, and those who minister to the congregation (members of the church choir). This distinction may not always apply to every local church because the team that leads praise and adoration may also be members of the church choir. The primary purpose of this office is to exalt, bless, honor and praise God and secondly, to minister to the church.

While worship is often not publicly expressed, praise is the "*sincere public acknowledgment of one's conviction that the Lord is worthy of honor and glory*". [67] A praise leader ministers to God with that conviction and leads the congregation to do the same during corporate worship. This conviction is usually expressed through singing, proclamation, dancing, clapping, etc.

The music ministry can be placed in the priestly ministry as well as the ministry of "*Helps*" (1 Cor. 12:28) or "*Ministries*" (Rom. 12:7). It is part of the priestly ministry because music ministers minister directly to God; by offering their bodies (Rom. 12:1), the fruit of their lips (Heb. 13:15-16), and leading the congregation to worship. As part of the *'helps or ministries'*, music ministers propagate the word of life (Act. 6:4) and minister in temporal affairs – ministering to the poor, needy, hurting, and down casts in the local church (Act. 6:1-3). That is to say, music ministers are also pastors, but of their team or departments. They are to take care of the needs of their members. In other words, music ministers are called, primarily, as ministers of God and then, ministers of men.

The office is a call from the Lord and not from man. It is not conferred on an individual by his or her pastor or church elder.

---

[67] (Pobee 2009)

It is a gift the Holy Spirit bestows on individuals as He wills. The ministry becomes evident in the life of an individual over time and is accepted by his/her local church. The pastor may lay hands on the individual to confirm or sharpen the gift; however, it is given by the Holy Spirit. The office is not just about putting together a few choruses and leading the people to sing them, or simply knowing how to play a musical instrument. It is a call that comes with so many demands. Just as every Christian is called to preach the Gospel but not everyone is called into the five-fold ministry, every Christian is called to praise God; however, not all Christians are called to be music ministers. We have all been called out of darkness into God's marvelous light and given a specific task to fulfill. That includes leading the church to praise God. We shall discuss this topic in much more detail in chapter six.

> *"But you are a chosen generation, a royal priesthood, a holy nation, His own special people; that you may proclaim the praises of Him who called you out of darkness into his marvelous light"* **1 Peter 2:9**

The office of a music minister is very sensitive because it requires holiness (Heb. 12:14). The minister must be sensitive to the Holy Spirit and not grief Him by how he/she lives. There are no shortcuts to living holy; the office makes no room for a *'wishy-washy'* kind of lifestyle, where one minute the minister is charged in the Spirit and the next moment, he/she is cold. It is an office that also requires watchfulness and discipline in your devotional and prayer life. It is also an office of trust because the people we lead are valuable in the sight of God – purchased with a high price, the precious blood of Christ. If you have the opportunity to usher them into the presence of God, you have to do so with reverence and awe. Music ministers ought to be people of virtues; honest, sincere, humble, and have a loving heart. They must learn to walk their talk but not be boastful. When the apostles were looking for people to serve in the

Members of the ministry have turned it into a 'university of vices', with fully developed 'departments of alcoholism, sexual perversion, gossips, busybodies and half-hearted Christians'.

helps ministry, in Acts chapter 6, their criteria included good reputation, full of the Holy Spirit, and wisdom, and these are some of the many qualities music ministers should have.

> *"³Therefore, brethren, seek out from among you seven men of good reputation, full of the Holy Spirit and wisdom, whom we may appoint over this business; ⁴ but we will give ourselves continually to prayer and to the ministry of the word."* **Acts 6:3-4**

The above scripture also alludes to the fact that music ministers should support the teaching and pastoral minister in the church. All the minister's activities and functions should reinforce the teachings of sound doctrine in the church, including the songs he/she sings.

Despite the glorious nature of the ministry, it is the most abused ministry in the church. For some reason, whenever something goes wrong in the church, it is connected to the music ministry; someone in the choir is always involved. Members of the ministry have turned it into a *'university of vices'*, with fully developed *'departments of alcoholism, sexual perversion, gossips, busybodies, and half-hearted Christians'*. As such, people have branded the ministry the most notorious ministry in the church. Those who stigmatize the ministry are not to be blamed because all manner of people have found their way into the ministry. I am not saying this derogatorily; I am a music minister too.

Since there are no entry requirements, the office has been besieged by proud and arrogant people; people who have no regard for authority. The department is very appealing to those who like drawing attention to themselves; people who have no business in the ministry. Those people used the ministry to promote their selfish interests rather than use it as a medium of ministering to God and the church. They have turned the office into a dolly on which they display their fashionable clothes. Such people also use their skills to bully their leaders with threats of leaving the local church if they do not have their way. I am not referring to ministers who leave the local church because of the deliberate attempts of leadership to suppress their ministry due to insecurity. Rather, I am referring to ministers who leave the local church because they were not allowed to use their position as music ministers to do the unacceptable.

Ministers of music should be teachable and ready to grow to a level where they will be sensitive to the Spirit of God; without which they will not adequately help the congregation attain the right level of fellowship with God.

The minister's calling should be evident to all. The fact that people can take up different responsibilities in the church does not mean they are called to be there. Similarly, the fact that someone can put two or three songs together and lead them powerfully, does not mean he/she qualifies to be a music minister. Some people may even have better singing voices, but that does not mean they have been molded for that office.

The music minister has to be spiritually sound. He/she should not be a baby in the Lord, for the reason that, the ministry requires a great deal of maturity. Ministers of music should be teachable and ready to grow to a level where they will be sensitive to the Spirit of God; without which they will not adequately help the congregation attain the right level of fellowship with God. This does not mean young Christians should not join the ministry, rather they have to give themselves to learning to grow to maturity. In some churches, an individual will not be allowed to lead in the church except they hold ministerial credentials, i.e., completed Bible college or about to complete one.

Again, I have disappointedly noticed that in many of the churches I have served, music ministers are the least respected.

There is very little understanding of the ministry among music ministers. Even most of the genuine ministers know very little about the office. Only a few ministers study the ministry or any related subject. Music is not just an art, it is also a science, therefore it must be studied. They need to know 'the dos and don'ts' of the ministry: how to develop their repertoire for ministration; how to prepare physically and spiritually for service; how to arrange their songs, how to introduce their songs, etc. They also need to know what to do when the Spirit of God is moving in the service; when to be silent and allow the Spirit of God to speak to the congregation by way of prophecy, word of wisdom, and word of knowledge, and when to raise a new song.

Again, I have disappointedly noticed that in many of the churches I have served, music ministers are the least respected. They are not consulted when decisions are made about the department. Pastors who like to micromanage the church will move people in and out of the department without adequately discussing it with the music minister. This, I feel is not right. On the other hand, when leadership is looking for someone to do menial jobs around the church, they will first look for the music minister, but, when it comes to performing honorable tasks, leadership will call other people. Whoever occupies the office of the music minister(s) should be accorded respect and dignity. Sadly, this is pushing a lot of genuine music ministers into the pastoral ministry or leaving the church completely, rather than staying to impact the world through their music. This is an unfortunate development!

In the remaining part of this chapter, we will learn about the qualities of a music minister. These qualities do not operate independently of the core Christian values, rather they are the additional qualities music ministers should have. These qualities are drawn from the life of David.

According to the ISBE, "*David was a many-sided man, with a character often at war with itself, a man with conflicting impulses, the flesh lusting against the spirit and the spirit against the flesh*".[68] Despite his limitations, every

---

[68] (James et al. 1939)

aspect of David's life provides great insights into how well we should worship our God. He dedicated a lot of the wealth he took from his enemies to God (2 Sam. 8:11) and initiated the use of psalms in worship, and he is known to have written 73 of the Psalms in the Bible. Thanks to him, the church uses music as one form of worship. David was a skillful musician, with a high sense of rhythm, an ear for pleasing sounds (1 Sam. 16:15-23), and he even invented some musical instruments (Amo. 6:5).

As a young man, he learned to trust and build himself in the Lord. The Lord also honored him with an eternal kingdom (2 Sam. 7:16) and bestowed upon him the title of Israel's chief musician and poet through the gift of prophetic inspiration. One of the greatest legacies is the qualities David possessed that earned him the title: *"the sweet psalmist of Israel"* (2 Sam. 23:1) because he knew God in a way that only a few men had ever known Him. These qualities can be placed in three groups, namely: the anointing, his skill, and character. Every music minister who wants to succeed in ministry must have these qualities.

> *"¹³Then Samuel took the horn of oil and anointed him in the midst of his brothers. And the Spirit of the LORD rushed upon David from that day forward. And Samuel rose up and went to Ramah. ¹⁴Now the Spirit of the LORD departed from Saul, and a harmful spirit from the LORD tormented him. ¹⁵And Saul's servants said to him, "Behold now, a harmful spirit from God is tormenting you.*

¹⁶Let our lord now command your servants who are before you to seek out a man who is skilful in playing the lyre, and when the harmful spirit from God is upon you, he will play it, and you will be well." ¹⁷So Saul said to his servants, "Provide for me a man who can play well and bring him to me." ¹⁸One of the young men answered, "Behold, I have seen a son of Jesse the Bethlehemite, who is skillful in playing, a man of valor, a man of war, pru-dent in speech, and a man of good presence, and the LORD is with him."

1 Samuel 16:13-18 ESV

1. The Anointing

The first most important quality David had that we need as individual music ministers, is the anointing. The anointing sanctifies or sets one apart for the master's use (Lev. 8:12). Before he was anointed, David lived in the shadows of his family. He was only a shepherd *"keeping the sheep of his father in the fields"* (1 Sam. 16:11). When Samuel the Prophet went to offer the Lord's sacrifice in his house, everyone was invited to the Lord's feast except David. When the feast was taking place in his father's house, he was not remembered. Out there, David was exposed to so many dangers (1 Sam. 17:34-35). He was exposed to the element of the harsh desert climate of Israel; he was at risk of

> *The first most important quality David had that we need as individual music ministers, is the anointing.*

dehydration, bites from dangerous reptiles, the attacks of lions and bears. He was even vulnerable to the attacks of bandits.

The question that comes to mind is: why was David left in the fields when there was such a great feast going on in his own father's house? The old Prophet was not only in town, but he was in David's house! What caused his father to forget him when he assembled his sons (1 Sam. 16:10-11)? The name David means well-beloved;[69] however, the action of his family indicated otherwise. Some theologians believe that David may have been born out of wedlock, and since Moses commanded that no one with such backgrounds should be allowed into the gatherings of God's people (Deu. 23:2), his family did not invite him to the Lord's feast (1 Sam. 16:3-5). These theologians support their argument with David's confession in Psalm 51:5 that his mother conceived him in sin and delivered him in guilt. Others believed that it was not deliberate; he was far from home at that time, so his family just allowed the function to move on without him. Whatever the issue was, God chose him to lead His people and from all indications, he lived up to God's expectations, despite his flaws, otherwise, God would not have promised him an everlasting kingdom (1 Chr. 17) through Christ Jesus the Messiah (Mat. 9:27).

---

[69] (Strong 2009, # H1732)

Before David was anointed, he was simply described as: *"ruddy, having beautiful eyes and good looks"* (1 Sam.16:12). Good looks and beautiful eyes alone are not enough to help you to fulfill the task God has given you, you need the anointing. The Bible says that after he was *"anointed in the midst of his brothers, the Spirit of the LORD rushed upon David from that day forward."* His description changed from *"ruddy young man with beautiful eyes and good looks"* to a *"skillful player, a man of valor, a man of war, prudent in speech, and a man of good presence, and someone the LORD was with"* (1 Sam. 16:13-18).

Good looks and beautiful eyes alone are not enough to help you to fulfill the task God has given you, you need the anointing.

The anointing broke the yoke of limitation upon his life (Isa. 10:27) and thrust him into the limelight. David became a super-star in one day (1 Sam. 17). The Lord took him from the dust, and lifted him from the dunghill, and set him among princes to inherit the throne of glory (1 Sam. 2:8). The anointing polished his talents and turned them into qualities that eventually took David into the palace of King Saul, the place he belonged. The anointing was his key to the supernatural, and without it, he would have lived an unaccomplished life.

Similarly, the anointing is the music minister's key to the supernatural. The minister can be the most learned, the most skilled, or the most talented, but the minister may not amount to anything until the minister is anointed. The minister may rise to stardom, travel the world, and do so many wonderful things, however, if he/she is not anointed, the fame and so-called good works will not last. The anointing for every office comes with its privileges (Num. 18:8) and demands (Lev. 10:7). It is important to note also that the anointing can be lost, so you need to stay connected to the source of your anointing. The anointing is given as the Spirit wills, therefore if you desire to operate in the office of a music minister, ask the Lord and be ready to pay the price for it but do not covert it because it might lead to your destruction (Act. 8:17-24; Act. 19:14-16).

2. Skill

> *Excellence represents the highest quality of a thing and our praise to God ought to be of the highest quality.*

Skill is the other quality music ministers should have. It is the knowledge and ability to do something well. It is not the same as talent, which is the natural gift or ability to do something. Talents are given by God, but skills are acquired. It could either be by formal education or by understudying someone. A talented person can become skillful by adding value to his/her talent. God expects us to improve the talents He has given us. Jesus in Matthew 25:14-30, told the parable of the talents where He made it clear that it is of essence to develop our talents.

Our God is a God of excellence (Psa. 8:1), therefore, whoever leads His people to praise Him, ought to do so with excellence. Excellence represents the highest quality and our praise to God ought to be of the highest quality. David's skill was the first quality that was noticed after he was anointed. Lack of skill does not only put people off during ministration, but it also hinders the move of God. A piece of music from an unskilled music minister sounds awkward in our ears, how much more in the ears of the Lord.

The minister needs to be skillful in the development of his/her repertoire for worship, in arranging his/her songs, and in ministering. His/her sensitivity to the move of God during ministration also needs skill. Playing an instrument skillfully and singing with the best vocal effect is as important as the minister's character and anointing. Christian music should be well produced and ministered to attract both believers and unbelievers alike. When skills are used together with the anointing of God, it can pull the world to Christ. Unfortunately, some of our Gospel music lack the skill needed to draw people into the kingdom.

As soon as you realize you have been called into the music ministry, take steps to improve your skills. If you think your calling is in the area of singing, for example, learn to play a musical instrument or two. There are so many skill development opportunities around these days, take advantage of them. Unlike the period I became a music minister, we did not have the internet, let alone YouTube, where we could freely watch and download songs. We had to play the cassettes of the songs we wanted to learn, pause them after every line, and write down the songs before we could learn to sing them. Thankfully, there are a lot of videos on the internet these days that can help music ministers sharpen their skills. Be wise Mr./Madam musician (Luke 16:8), use the resources the world offers to enrich the kingdom. Also, ask the Lord to give you a creative mind and heart to lead His people into his presence in worship.

> *"Do you see a man skillful in his work? He will stand before kings; he will not stand before obscure men".* **Proverb 22:29 ESV**

Creativity springs from the desire for change; the craving for something new. If you are not skillful in a field of ministry, study, or profession, you cannot explore other ways of doing the same thing because you do not know.

Skill will always create opportunities for you to go places and meet people of prominence. There are a lot of talented people in this world who cannot go far in ministry because they do not develop their skills. Skill is the hallmark of creativity. Creativity is about careful consideration and planning. It aims at getting the best and acceptable result. Creativity springs from the desire for change; the craving for something new. If you are not skillful in a field of ministry, study, or profession, you cannot explore other ways of doing the same thing because you do not know. If you do not have the skill to know and try different methods, how can you get the best result?

> *"Sing unto him a new song; play skilfully with a loud noise."* **Psalm 33:3**

David was driven by the anointing and skills to do exploits in his generation for God. He was never satisfied with the way he praised God, so he always looked for different ways to praise the Lord. He wrote that *"But I will hope continually and will yet praise thee more and more"* (Psa. 71:14). Again, he said in Psalm 119:164 *"Seven times a day do I praise thee because of thy righteous judgments."* It takes skill to be able to praise God this much. If he was not skillful, he would not have been able to transform worship the way he did in his days.

> *Our talents are like seeds that need to be sown in the soil of knowledge so they can yield the desired outputs.*

In the part of the world that I come from, most people rely solely on their talents and make very little effort to improve their skills in the art of making music. Our talents are like seeds that need to be sown in the soil of knowledge so it can yield the desired output (Mat. 25:14-30). The Lord expects us to turn those talents into useful skills. It is important not to let our skills take the best of us. It is supposed to be used to honor the Lord. People who are blessed with great talents and skills usually become very arrogant. They forget that they are where they are because the Lord made it possible. They fail to recognize that they are only custodians of the Father's gifts. Do not allow your skills to destroy you!

3. Character

Although skill is very important, it is not as important as the character of the music minister. Skill can make you famous within a very short time; however, you need a godly character to keep you at the top for a long time. A bad character may even destroy the anointing upon your life. Many skillful people rise to the top and fall suddenly because they did not have what it takes to stay at the top. No matter how rich or successful you become, when you do not have the right character, you will lose everything in a short time. David had what it took to keep him at the top, despite his shortcomings.

"If your character and reputation were to meet in the dark, will they recognize each other as coming from the same person?"

David went through similar character training before God finally put him on the throne. It was the character David developed that made him spare the life of Saul when he had opportunities to kill him (1 Sam. 24:3). Rev. Phiri once asked my cohort of Bible school students *"if your character and reputation were to meet in the dark, will they recognize each other as coming from the same person?"* Character is the most important of all the qualities.

For most people, as soon as they get the anointing, they want to go out there and *"do the work of God!"* Sometimes the Lord may delay your rise in your ministry because He wants you to build the desired character before releasing you to prominence. The anointing upon your life and God's love may just be restraining you from destruction. The fact that you have received the anointing does not mean you are ready for the task ahead of you. Character development is needed, otherwise, the minister will end up consuming the flock of God rather than feeding them (Act. 20:28; 1 Pet. 5:2).

After David was anointed, he did not parade himself for the town to know, rather he returned to his normal duties until it was time for him to go into the palace of Saul. Before then, he knew it was not time for his exposure, so he carefully kept his anointing secret. The work of the Spirit upon his life could not be hidden for a long time; it made him shine in obscurity to the point that all his neighbors observed with wonder the great improvements in his life. Even in his shepherd's garb, David became a champion. Below is an exposition on the character traits of David that made him a model for all worship leaders.

a. A Man of Valor

The word valor has many meanings; however, for this book, I have used courage and boldness. This is not the type that is arrogant, boastful, or contentious. This courage is humble and obedient; an essential character trait every music minister should have. 1 Thessalonians 2:2 says "...*we were bold in our God*..." That is the mark of a man of valor! The music ministry is not for timid people. God usually directs us to fulfill His purpose in ways people may not understand or agree with; anytime we step outside the usual boundaries, we stand the risk of being rejected. However, we should not allow that to keep us from doing the will of God. A point in time when David used his boldness against a critic of his style of worship was when Michal criticized him for dancing in public before the returning Ark of the Covenant (2 Sam. 6:16-23).

Sometimes the expression on the faces of the congregation can be very intimidating, especially when you are not familiar with them. It is often not a deliberate attempt by them to intimidate you. For most people, the church is the only place they can run to for comfort; a place they will not be judged, so they come with all their problems. You need the courage to be able to tell them: "*it is well*" in the midst of

Sometimes things may not be going well with you, but you need to put your problems aside and encourage the congregation to praise God.

their problems. You need the courage to get them into the mood to praise God despite their challenges. Sometimes it can be so bad that people become indifferent during service. You may even encounter an elder who is keen on maintaining the '*traditions of the church*' and will go to great lengths to hinder the occurrence of anything new during worship. This is when boldness is of the essence because it makes the congregation believe you know what you are doing (Act. 4:13) so they follow you confidently to worship.

Boldness enables you to stand up against falsehood and it is an antidote to fear (2 Tim. 1:7). It helps you tell it as it is. Sometimes things may not be going well with you, but you need to put your problems aside and encourage the congregation to praise God. This is one of the reasons why God allows us to experience trials so we can encourage other people (2 Cor. 1:3-4). Boldness is a gift of God (Act. 4:29); an inheritance of the children of God (Dan. 11:32). It is needed to enter the presence of God (Eph. 3:12; Heb. 10:19).

I started my music ministry at a time when there was a lot of misunderstanding about the use of contemporary music and musical instrument in worship, particularly in the traditional churches, like the one I grew up in. The older folks were used to singing from the church's hymnal, so the idea of rising to their feet, clapping, singing, and dancing to choruses led by a group of teenagers to the sound of the jazz drum, piano, and guitars during worship, was foreign to a lot of them, hence, they resisted every attempt to have us use contemporary music in church. I had just completed high school at that time where we used those instruments and we saw nothing wrong with them. The youth who could not stand and fight for the cause left the church in droves to the then-emerging charismatic churches, where the use of those instruments was accepted. This was a sad development because the church had invested in these youths and trained them to the level where they could take up leadership roles, but because of the elders' unwillingness to embrace change, we lost them to other churches.

Those of us who did not want to leave decided to fight for the cause. We identified a few elders who were young at heart and could lobby other elders to allow us to purchase those instruments to use during service. The initial discussion did not go well because the idea was seriously resisted by the hard-liners. After prolonged lobbying, we were given the green light to raise funds to purchase a few instruments, but with a lot of conditions. After we bought the instruments and dedicated them for use, our next battle was to get the older folks to participate in the praises we led. I was one of the leaders spear-heading the change and the one who led praises, so I had to be very circumspect in the way I carried myself on stage; my gestures and words. I sometimes had to deliberately avoid looking at the faces of some of the elders when I led praises to avoid being distracted by the stern look on their faces. Over time, I began to see those elders who initially resisted the idea fully participating and dancing to our music, praise God!

Looking back today, I realized that God gave us a lot of boldness in the face of the many oppositions we faced in raising a praise team for the church. I am really grateful to God because I could have easily given in to the many pressures and distractions we faced in those days, thank God for the boldness to believe in and stay the cause!

b. A Man of War

Under the Old Covenant, people had to fight to get and defend what belonged to them. Under the New Covenant, to be a man of war means to be a prayerful believer. He/she must be able to stand alone in prayer. By the office and the anointing upon the minister, he/she has to be "*a man or a woman of war;*" otherwise, they will not survive the fiery darts of the enemy (Eph. 6:16). Ministering is more of a spiritual exercise than physical activity. It demands discipline and self-control.

Since the devil knows the benefits of getting into that realm, he does all he can to hinder that from happening, and the music minister becomes a target of the enemy.

The life of David gives us enough examples to prop up the idea of standing alone in prayer. When he arrived at the battlefield where the battle between Israel and the Philistine was going to take place, his brother vehemently opposed him. When he was brought to Saul, he was clothed with ammunition he could not function with. After God helped him to kill Goliath, all hell broke loose against him. He became an instant enemy of Saul, who made several attempts to kill him (1 Sam. 23:7-28; 24:1-22). He was forced to live a life of a fugitive; living in caves (1 Sam. 22:1-2; 24:3), in foreign lands (1 Sam. 22:3), and attacked by foreign forces (1 Sam. 30:1-6). He was ridiculed by Nabal (1 Sam. 25:10-11), had to pretend to be insane (1 Sam. 21:12-15), and at a point, he became so hungry that he had to eat the sacred bread that was reserved for only the priests (1 Sam. 21:6); but through it all, he learned to pray and trust in God.

There is a realm of consciousness in God's presence that is only attained by abiding in Christ, [70] and as a worship leader, you need to know how to get there and help the congregation to do the same. Since the devil knows the benefits of getting into that realm, he does all he can to hinder that from happening, and the music minister becomes a target of the enemy. The minister, therefore, needs to be on a constant watch against the devil. Someone once said, *"we are part-time Christians fighting a full-time devil."* The devil never gives up, so why should we? In 1 Peter 5:8, the Apostle Peter says:

> *"Be sober, be vigilant; because your adversary*
> *the devil, as a roaring lion, walketh about,*
> *seeking whom he may devour."*

Sometimes, the storms of life get so overwhelming; you feel down, discouraged, and just want to give up because nothing seems to be working in your life. Friends may not even be there to stand with you in prayer and the people you trust may even not be picking your calls. That is when you need to go down on your knees and pray for God to come to your aid. You also need to learn to *"encourage yourself in the Lord,"* like David did (1 Sam. 30:6).

Until recently, I never knew that most of the attacks and battles that I faced were a result of the anointing upon my life. I encountered unimaginable challenges and felt like quitting so many times. I remember asking myself on many occasions whether it was worth the struggles. In those moments, I learned to stand on my own in prayer because I had no one to turn to

---

[70] (Pobee 2009)

Until recently, I never knew that most of the attacks and battles that I faced were a result of the anointing upon my life. I faced unimaginable challenges and sometimes felt like quitting.

but my God. Little did I know that God was preparing me for a great music ministry. I thank God for those moments because if things had not been so, I would not have had so much knowledge and experience to share with you.

Now I know how to go to God in prayer and how important it is for me to keep praying more than ever before. I know where to turn to for help in times of need. It has not been easy, but God is good. I know a lot of other music ministers who have suffered life-threatening attacks because of the anointing upon their lives. But thank God because He only allows the devil up to the point we can bear.

Whenever you lift your voice in praise, you tell the devil that Yahweh is the only God in the universe and that makes you his target. It gets even worse when your worship brings a sinner to Christ. Satan looks for opportunities to get back at you. You need to be on your prayer tower at all times. The most important information you need in such moments is to '*stay connected to your source of strength.*'

c. Prudent in Speech

Prudence in speech (eloquence) refers to the ability to choose and use words (the word of God) in a manner that will edify, encourage, and comfort your hearers (Rom. 14:19; 1 Cor. 10:23, 14:3; Eph. 4:29; Col. 4:6). It means using your words in

a manner that will save you from trouble and prolong your life
(Pro. 18:21; 1 Pet. 3:10). It also refers to the number of words,
kind of words, and manner (tone, facial expression) in which
you use your words, whether ministering or not.

> *"For in many things we offend all. If any man
> offends not in word, the same is a perfect man,
> and able also to bridle the whole body."*
> **James 3:2**

The King James Version (KJV) translates this quality as: *"prudent in matters."* David was wise because he knew how to behave in his conversation, conduct, and behavior, especially in King Saul's court (1 Sam 18: 5, 14, 30). This is evidence of heavenly wisdom, no wonder he eventually made it to the throne.

Prudent in matters is not about manipulating or intimidating people, telling lies in the name of positive confession, or cracking unnecessary jokes.

Prudence in matters is not about manipulating or intimidating people, telling lies in the name of positive confession, or cracking unnecessary jokes (Mat. 12:36; Luk. 12:47). It is not being a babbler, double-tongued, gossipper, or quarrelsome (Ecc. 10:11; 1 Tim. 3:3, 8).

When employed during corporate worship, prudence in speech puts the minds of the congregation at ease, by appealing to and motivating them to praise God. A prudence speech captures every mind-boggling thought about the ability of God and keeps the minds of the congregation on God. The minister needs to develop the habit of studying and meditating on the word of God daily (Jos. 1:8; Psa. 119:11). Music ministers should also be careful about the kinds of words that come out of their mouths because they occupy a position of influence.

d. A Man of Good Presence

To be a man or woman of good presence refers to dressing decently, yet modestly. It is the quality of commanding respect by always looking good, wearing a smile, being approachable, and being likable. It refers to dressing in a way that will not take the people's attention away from Jesus. This does not mean you should use the glory of God and humility as excuses to dress shabbily. If you adopt any of the above extreme cases: people will either get infuriated at your appearance and not partake in worship or they will be carried away by your dressing and will spend the time stirring and talking about you rather than worshiping.

You are standing on that stage because of Jesus; therefore, all attention should be on Him. When you dress anyhow, people will not take you seriously and they will not partake in worship to get blessed. Be in your best and at your best when ministering to the Lord. There is something peculiar and attractive about music ministers who are serious about their relationship with God. As a result of their genuine intimacy with the Lord, they are clothed with so much glory. It is inexplicable! People are easily attracted to them. They worship the Lord in a way that causes people to desire to do what they do and even be their friends.

"Praise ye the LORD: for it is good to sing praises unto our God; for it is pleasant, and praise is comely." **Psalm 147:1**

"Rejoice in the LORD, O ye righteous: for praise is comely for the upright." **Psalm 33:1**

e. The Lord is with Him

The final character trait that David had was that the Lord was with him. To say *'the Lord is with someone'* means the person's ways please Him. His/her life is blessed, although not devoid of challenges. The person may not be the most anointed, the most talented, the best looking, or the most eloquent but when the Lord is with the person, it changes everything in his/her favor. Every minister's aim should be to let their way please the Lord.

"When a man's ways please the LORD, he maketh even his enemies to be at peace with him." **Proverb 16:7**

The most important quality of all is the continuous dwelling of God's presence in one's life. God's continuous presence guarantees victory over sin and the devil. This is what the Bible calls having *"favor with both God and man"* (Luk. 2:52). If the Lord delights in your ways, He will make it successful. Since the office of a music minister is spiritual, yet operates in a physical domain, the devil is always against you. Therefore, if the Lord is not with you, you will not survive his rate of attacks.

You need to have the presence of God dwelling with you at all times.

> *"For a day in thy courts is better than a thousand. I had rather be a doorkeeper in the house of my God than to dwell in the tents of wickedness."* **Psalm 84:10**

Never forget, you did not assume that office because you are the most qualified or the worthiest. You are there because God chose to put you there for His pleasure. Give Him all the pleasure He desires, and He will never depart from you. David asked the Lord never to cast him away from his presence (Psa. 51:11) because he knew that his very life depended on Him and that without Him, he could do nothing (Joh. 15:5).

Prayer

May God help you develop the qualities needed to be the Lord's vessel of honor.

I will, in the next chapter, look at the duties of music ministers.

Chapter 6

The Duties of Music Ministers

Tここ here should be a pattern music ministers follow when
ministering. Music ministers can function efficiently and
effectively if they know what their duties are. The writer of the
book of Hebrews stated that:

> *"Who serve unto the example and shadow of*
> *heavenly things, as Moses was admonished of*
> *God when he was about to make the taber-*
> *nacle: for, See, saith he, that thou make all*
> *things according to the pattern shewed to thee*
> *in the mount."* **Hebrews 8:5**

If the tabernacle of worship that Moses was instructed to
build followed the pattern showed him on the mountain and the
priests also ministered according to the pattern given to Moses,
which were all shadows of the real glory that was revealed in
Christ, then there must be a pattern music ministers need to
follow because we are worshipping the same God of the Bible,

Music ministers will be great sources of inspiration and guidance to their department, as well as contribute to the growth and development of the local church if they can identify their duties and the pattern with which they are called to minister.

but under a better covenant (Heb. 8:7-12).

Unlike the people under the Old Covenant whose instructions were written on tablets of stone; external, our instructions are written on the tablets of our hearts and administered by the Holy Spirit who dwells in us. That is the more reason why we need to spend time with God for Him to teach us how to worship Him and lead our local church to do the same. Music ministers will be great sources of inspiration and guidance to their department, as well as contribute to the growth and development of the local church if they would spend time with the Holy Spirit to show them what their duties are. As already mentioned, ministering is not just about selecting a few songs and leading them during corporate worship, it is all about doing the will of the Lord. We need to know what God wants us to do, how to do it, and when to do it. Nothing is more important in your ministration than these three things.

We need to know what God wants us to do, how to do it, and when to do it during our ministration. Nothing is more important in your ministration than these three things.

In the ensuing pages, I have outlined and discussed the general duties of music ministers in much detail. Although the list may not be exhaustive and may vary between congregations,

I believe this discussion will guide music ministers and help them to improve their ministration.

1. Ministering to God

The first and most important duty of music ministers is their devotion to the Lord. You cannot minister to the Lord if you are not devoted to Him. This is because you minister directly to God. Every minister should cultivate daily habits that will foster a deeper relationship with God. I am not just talking about daily Bible readings and prayer, but about developing an intimate relationship with God that comes only by spending time with Him. Every activity that takes place in the ministry is important, but nothing is as important as the minister's relationship with God.

The minister's relationship with God should not just be about preparing for the next ministration; it should include spending time alone with God doing nothing other than listening to Him. After feeding 5,000 people with five loaves of bread and two fishes in Matthew 14:13-21, He sent His disciples to cross the Sea of Galilee by boat while He dismissed the crowd (Mat. 14:22). *"And when He had sent the multitudes away, He went up on the mountain by Himself to pray. Now when evening came, He was alone there."* (v. 23 NKJV). If the Lord Jesus, who is the son of God, saw the need to be alone with His Father, how much more do we need a daily time of solitude to pour out our hearts to God, ponder His Word, and prepare to follow His directions.

This kind of relationship with God is developed through discipline and faithfully keeping a strict routine. Paraphrasing

David McCasland's devotional, he stated that to wait on the Lord, we need a quiet room – anywhere we can focus on the Lord with little or no distractions, an empty page – a receptive mind, a blank sheet of paper, and a willingness to listen while asking the Lord 'is there something You want me to know and waiting for the Lord to speak to you by His Holy Spirit, His Word, and with the assurance of His direction. [71]

Our failure to walk closely with God will not only rob us, as music ministers of strength and inspiration but will ultimately, deny the congregation of the divine experience that accompanies corporate worship. It is said that *"you cannot lead someone to a place you have never gone before."* Similarly, you cannot lead others to have fellowship with God if you don't have continuous fellowship with Him. Walking closely with God deepens the minister's revelation and understanding of Him.

2. Creating the Atmosphere for Fellowship

The minister ushers the congregation into the presence of God by singing songs of praise and adoration that create an atmosphere suitable for the Spirit of God to meet with the congregation.

The second duty of the music minister is to create an atmosphere for the congregation to worship and have fellowship with God. The minister ushers the congregation into the presence of God by singing songs of praise and adoration that create an atmosphere suitable for the Spirit of God to meet with them.

---

[71] (McCasland 2014)

All external expressions of worship; singing, dancing, lifting of hands, and kneeling contribute to creating that atmosphere, and ministers should encourage them. Time is a key ingredient when creating the atmosphere for fellowship and ministers may sometimes exceed their allotted time. The host (the person conducting the service), on the other hand, may sometimes be tempted to interrupt the praise and worship to move on to other activities; nevertheless, when ministers know what God wants to do that day and listen attentively while ministering, they will fulfill the purpose of the day's ministration within the allocated time. However, ministers should not make it a practice of exceeding their allotted time in the name of allowing God to meet with His people in fellowship. Ministers should focus on creating the right atmosphere and leave the rest to God.

When ministers know what God wants to do that day and listen attentively while ministering, they will fulfill the purpose of the day's ministration within the allocated time.

After the congregation has successfully entered the chamber of God, the minister should use the appropriate song(s) to welcome the glory of God. Once the minister senses that the Spirit of God is ready to minister to His people, the minister should step aside for the presence of God to take over the service. This, in my opinion, is the peak of every worship service, when the people groan in the Spirit, weep, prostrate, kneel, remain silent, and love the Lord, while God ministers to them. This period of fellowship is the most important and sacred part of the entire service because God meets the people individually.

It is, however, very easy to miss this part of the service simply due to the music minister's insensitivity.

The minister should be spiritually mature to know how to create the right atmosphere for worship and when to step aside. Leading the saints to worship God requires a high level of sensitivity, which is attained through building a strong relationship with God – by continually staying in the presence of God through prayer, fasting, Bible studies, and living a life of purity. It demands a life of sacrifice and total devotion.

After the dedication of the Temple by Solomon, the Levites sang and played their instruments in thanks and praise to God to the point where the priests could not minister. The glory of God filled the Temple and took over the service. This should occur during every gathering of the saints of God. God should be in the helms of affairs.

> *"13It came even to pass, as the trumpeters and singers were as one, to make one sound to be heard in praising and thanking the LORD; and when they lifted up their voice with the trumpets and cymbals and instruments of music, and praised the LORD, saying, For he is good; for his mercy endureth for ever: that then the house was filled with a cloud, even the house of the LORD; 14So that the priests could not stand to minister by reason of the cloud: for the glory of the LORD had filled the house of God."* **2 Chronicles 5:13-14**

Before I move on to the next topic, let me share a little experience on this topic with you. I was the assistant praise team leader for the Methodist-Presbyterian Union (MPU), a Christian fellowship for those of us from the Methodist and Presbyterian tradition at the University of Ghana. That was during my undergraduate days. We had an annual praise festival known as 'Sing O Praise,' which was a service set aside for just praise and it was about an hour long. It was usually held on the last Sunday before our final exams for the semester. All the members of the fellowship looked forward to this festival and the team also prepared enthusiastically for it.

The Methodist-Presbyterian Union (MPU) had a yearly rotational leadership tradition, for one academic year, the Presbyterians would occupy the top positions in the union and the Methodists would assist. The following academic year, the order would reverse. I was serving as the assistant praise team leader for the year in question and I was a Methodist. Interestingly, in the praise team that year, the leader and the vice were both Methodists.

Before the festival, the praise team leader, who was an executive member of the Union's governing body, had to present the team's final plan for the festival at their meeting so that other executive members could make inputs. When our leader mentioned that the program will be an hour-long as we've always had it, the evangelism secretary (ES), who was the person in charge of programs, said she had planned that the fellowship would have communion on that day as well. And considering how long it took to serve communion, she had cut down the festival time to just 30 minutes instead of our usual one hour. This change in plans sparked a lengthy debate at the executive meeting that evening and drag the meeting way beyond the usual time. But at the end of the meeting, our leader could not prevail because the evangelism secretary (ES) stood her ground and would not budge because the final decision about programs rested with her.

When my leader informed me, I suggested that we meet with the ES privately and tried to convince her as I felt that she wanted to appear strong at the meeting. When we met with her, we tried to explain how hard we had been working towards the program; planning, rehearsing, advertising, praying, and fasting for almost a year. But she was stuck in her heels. I remember she said, "I don't even know why I am talking to you", which was to me, "you are not an executive member so you should not get involved in this discussion." I felt very offended by that comment, and I told my leader that we should forget it.

As we walked away, I just sensed in my spirit that this was the devil at work, trying to demoralize us. I turned to my leader and told him that we needed to fast and pray in the next three weeks so that God will show up and perform a miracle that has never been heard of in the Union. I believed that the devil wanted to prevent us from receiving God's blessings and the only way he could be defeated was to pray for God's intervention. For those three weeks, my leader and I fasted and met every evening to pray for the festival. A week before the festival, we asked the team to join us in the fast. Our prayer during those three weeks was "God show your glory and silence any program of hell against Your festival."

The night before the festival, we had our final rehearsal and prayer time. During prayer, a member of the team gave us a Word of Knowledge. It was simple but very profound, "Be still and know that I am the Lord, I will show my glory in your midst." The team was so encouraged by that word, and we all returned to our rooms with joy and peace in our hearts. We also changed the order of our ministration for that day. Previously, we opened the festival with upbeat songs (which we called praises) and then move to the slow beat songs (which we called worship) in the second half of the ministration. That day, we opened the festival with the slow-tempo songs, which I led, and we ended with the upbeat songs, which our team leader led.

About 15 minutes into my ministration, the glory of God descended so strongly in the auditorium that no one could stay on their feet. The entire congregation was down on their knees and some people laid prostrate before the Lord. People were praising God so loudly that it almost felt chaotic. Others were also confessing their sins. I am talking about a congregation of a little over 500 university students. We were simply drunk with the Holy Spirit!

When I realized that, I ask the team to stop singing and just allow the keyboardist to play the songs as we worshipped. At a point, I felt led to ask the congregation to remain silent before the Lord and just listen for His voice as He moved in the auditorium. The glory of God was so strong that I felt His embrace; it felt like a bear hug, so weighty. I just stepped aside and allowed the Spirit of God to have His way. Words cannot fully describe my experience that day; my best description is that it was awesome, simply out of this world! God showed up that day and changed our lives.

When we were done with our ministration, the congregation wanted more, and they were not happy that the festival was cut short to make way for communion. Everyone looked forward to the day and they felt very disappointed at the decision to serve communion. They were, however, very happy to have had that encounter with God. At the end of the service, the ES felt very bad that she was so adamant about having a communion service that day. She even apologized to our leader. No ES, from that day, ever attempted to plan any other program on the festival day; it was just for praise.

I learned an important lesson that day; God loves to be praised and when we learn to wait on God, create the atmosphere for fellowship, and allow Him to lead us in ministration, He always shows up and does extraordinary things. He loves it when His children set their hearts on pleasing Him.

The Presence and the Glory of God

Is there a difference between the Presence and the Glory of God? Is the Omnipresence different from the Presence of God? Although the Omnipresence, the Presence, and the Glory of God are all related, they are three distinct concepts. This differentiation is not only meant to inform you but also to encourage you to desire the glory of God above everything else in your life.

a. The Presence of God (Yahweh)

The Presence of God can be described as the awareness or consciousness of God. When one enters the presence of God, it means the person has entered His dwelling place; the courts, where God resides. Can one go into the dwelling place of God but not have His attention? Yes, I believe so; you can be in someone's presence and not have the person's attention.

Once upon a time, the people of Israel took the Ark of God (the Presence of God) to the battlefield but were defeated by the Philistines.

> *"³And when the people were come into the camp, the elders of Israel said, Wherefore hath the LORD smitten us today before the Philistines? Let us fetch the ark of the covenant of the LORD out of Shiloh unto us, that, when it cometh among us, it may save us out of the hand of our enemies... ⁵And when the ark of the covenant of the LORD came into the camp, all Israel shouted with a great shout, so that the earth rang again.⁶And when the Philistines heard the noise of the shout, they said, What meaneth the noise of this great shout in the camp of the Hebrews? And they understood that the ark of the LORD was come into the camp...¹⁰And the Philistines fought, and Israel was smitten, and they fled every man into his tent: and there was a very great slaughter; for there fell of Israel thirty thousand footmen. ¹¹And the ark of God was taken; and the two sons of Eli, Hophni and Phinehas, were slain."* **1 Samuel 4:3, 5-6, 10-11**

The presence of God was there but His glory had departed (1 Sam 4:2s1) because the nation had sinned. Since the Ark of the Covenant represented the presence of Yahweh in the nation of Israel, once the glory had departed, they only had a dead

Ark. This means it is the glory of God that gives meaning and essence to the presence.

It is not sufficient to live only in the presence of God, but one needs the higher dimension; which is the Glory of God.

The presence of God is not tangible but inferred or experienced, yet it exists. It represents an aspect of His personality but not His entirety. For instance, I may be at home but not available to everyone who walks into the house. This does not mean God is not aware of His surroundings. The ISBE states "*the presence of God represents His preposition,*" [72] that is, a part of His personality. Living in the presence alone is not enough because it is not the fullness of God.

The first Hebrew word that speaks of God's presence is "*min minniy minney*", and it is translated as "*a part of*", which prepositionally means "*from or out of*". [73] The second Hebrew word which speaks of God's presence is "*paniym*", and it is also translated as "*the face; a preposition (before), favor, in or out of the sight of, forefront, heaviness*". [74] Other scriptures in which these two Hebrew words have been translated to mean the presence of God includes Genesis 3:8; Exodus 33:14; Psalm 16:11; Psalm 95:2; Isaiah 63:9, etc. The Greek word translated to mean the presence of God is "*enopion*", which also means "*in the face of, i.e., before, in the presence (sight) of.*"[75] The word '*presence*' as used in the verses above is translated from both words "*min minniy minney and paniym*" (Hebrew) and

---

[72] (James et al. 1939)

[73] (Strong 2009, # H4480)

[74] (Strong 2009, # H6440)

[75] (Strong 2009, # G1799)

"*enopion*" (Greek), both refer to an aspect of God's disposition but not a complete description of His entirety. It goes to say that it is not sufficient to live only in the presence of God, but one needs the higher dimension; which is the Glory of God.

> *"And the angel answering said unto him, I am Gabriel, that stand in the presence of God; and am sent to speak unto thee, and to shew thee these glad tidings."* **Luke 1:19**

Does this mean there is a difference between the Omnipresence and the Presence of God? I would say, sure, there is a difference! The word, "*omnipresence*" does not appear in the Bible, however, according to the ISBE, "*it speaks of God's presence with reference to the pervasive immanence of His being. It frequently contents itself with affirming the universal extent of God's power and knowledge.*" [76] Paul the Apostle wrote about the omnipresence of God.

> *"For the invisible things of him from the creation of the world are clearly seen, being understood by the things that are made, even his eternal power and Godhead; so that they are without excuse"* **Romans 1: 20**

The word Omnipresence has two components: i.e., God is '*everywhere* and *present*'–divine presence. This means the presence and operation of God are not limited by space or time. It is the general presence of God that is available to both the

---

[76] (James et al. 1939)

righteous and the unrighteous. However, the presence of God, as mentioned above, refers to the aspect of God's personality that is accessible to only believers. Some of the Bible verses that refer to God's omnipresence are Psalm 139:6-16; Proverbs 15:3; Jeremiah 23:23-24; Amos 9:2; 1 Kings 8:27; 2 Chronicles 2:6; and Isaiah 66:1.

b. The Glory of God (Yahweh)

It is only in genuine worship that one can experience the Glory of God. The Glory of God represents His attendance or His occupancy. The Hebrew word translated as the Glory of God is "*kabod*," which means "*weight, in a sense of splendor or copiousness: i.e, glory and honor.*" [77] The word "*Kabod*" comes from another Hebrew verb "*kabad kabed*", which means "*to be heavy, that is, in number, riches or honor.*"[78] The Greek word translated as glory is the word "*Doxa*". "*Doxa*" means "*dignity, glory(-ious), honor, praise, worship.*"[79] The Brown-Driver-Briggs' Hebrew Definitions add: "*abundance, reputation, and reverence*"[80] to the meaning of the word "*Doxa.*"

Interestingly, the Greek word "*doxa*" has also been translated to mean praise and worship – not only singing and dancing but living a life that pleases God. This adds credence to the fact that it is only in genuine worship that one can experience the glory of God. True worship is the purpose of all creation and

---

[77] (Strong 2009, # H3519)

[78] (Strong 2009, # H3513)

[79] (Strong 2009, # G1391)

[80] (Brown, Driver, and Briggs 1976)

when creation (particularly humans) fulfill this purpose, God is pleased, and He attends their gathering with the weightiness of His presence. The glory is far greater than the Presence of God.

> *"And it came to pass, as Aaron spake unto the whole congregation of the children of Israel that they looked toward the wilderness, and, behold, the glory of the LORD appeared in the cloud."* **Exodus 16:10**

> *"And then shall appear the sign of the Son of man in heaven: and then shall all the tribes of the earth mourn, and they shall see the Son of man coming in the clouds of heaven with power and great glory."* **Matthew 24:30**

> *"¹The heavens declare the glory of God and the firmament sheweth his handywork. ²Day unto day uttereth speech, and night unto night sheweth knowledge. ³There is no speech nor language, where their voice is not heard."*
> **Psalm 19:1-3**

When God created humankind, He clothed them with glory and honor (Psa. 8:5). But mankind chose to turn them over to the devil (Gen. 3:6; Rom. 3:23) and the glory and honor of humanity were stolen. Under the Old Covenant, only the High Priests could experience the glory (Exo. 40:33-35; Lev. 9:23).

The glory is what the Jews refer to as the *"Shechinah"*- the dwelling. Although the term is not found in the Bible, *"it has been borrowed by Christians, to express the visible majesty of the divine Presence, especially when resting or dwelling between the cherubim on the Mercy-Seat, in the Tabernacle, and the Temple of Solomon, but not in the Second Temple. The idea conveyed is that of the most brilliant and glorious light, enveloped in a cloud, and usually concealed by the cloud, so that the cloud itself was, for the most part, alone visible, but on particular occasions, the glory appeared".* [81]

The appearance of the glory of God is supposed to be the pinnacle of every corporate worship. Whenever the church gathers, the glory of God should be present. Unfortunately, the glory of God is rarely experienced in the present-day church. This has made the church dry and empty; filled with *"the blind, lame, disfigured, deformed, the broken-footed, the broken-handed, the crook-backed, crushed ones, those with a blemish in his eye, the scurvy, the scabbed and those with crushed testicles"* (Lev. 21:18-20 MKJV).

Why is the glory of God absent from our churches? Why are we not experiencing the glory of God like the men of old? I will attempt to answer these questions solely based on the experiences I have had from the places I have ministered at.

i. We often do not gather unto the Lord. Our gathering is usually to raise funds, to listen to an invited preacher or our pastor, to show our new clothing and other accessories, to see our friends, or finish a conversation we did not complete. We do not gather with the sole reason of thanking, praising, and worshipping the Lord.

---

[81] (Smith 2016)

Solomon gathered the nation in Jerusalem to dedicate the Temple and the vessels and offer sacrifices to God (2 Chr. 5:2, 5). Since the gathering was unto God, He was in attendance. During our church services, we say and do so many things other than fellowship with Jesus. We sing about so many things other than about Christ (1 Cor. 2:2). Our churches are not growing because we have failed to lift Christ (Joh. 12:32). The offering of our life (Rom. 12:1) and the fruits of our lips (Heb. 13:15) are the only things that bring down the glory of God. If these are missing from our gatherings, the glory of God will never be in attendance.

ii. The glory of God is rarely experienced in our gatherings because the people who lead the church in worship often do not sanctify themselves. Ministers have to keep themselves for that solemn moment of meeting with God. Until we learn to sanctify ourselves we will not experience the Glory of God in our gatherings (Jos. 3:5; 2 Chr. 30:3, 8).

It is also recorded that the priests *"...did not then wait by course:"* (2 Chr. 5:11). According to 1 Chronicles 24, David had introduced a rotational system of weekly service, which was intended for the ordinary duties of the priesthood and not for a great occasion such as the dedication of the Temple of God. Our worship services are greater than the dedication of Solomon's Temple because those ceremonies were shadows of the 'real deal'; the dispensation of the church under the administration of the Holy Spirit. In other words, the glory of

God interrupted their routine, and there was no room for ordinary duties but miracles. When we wait on God before ministration, every service will be a miracle service.

Sadly, after that great dedication ceremony, the glory of God never showed up again in the nation of Israel in their post-wilderness life until Pentecost. For us the New Testament church, this visitation is supposed to be a weekly if not a daily occurrence. However, the glory of God continues to elude us because sanctification and holiness are no longer valued by the church.

Sanctification in the life of an individual is attained by yielding to the Lord, living holy, praying (Luk. 6:12, Col. 4:2), fasting (Deu. 10:20-21), and studying the Bible (Psa. 119:11; Joh. 17:17). Remember the Lord is holy (1 Sam. 2:2) and He only inhabits holy praise (Psa. 22:3). A lot of praise leaders either live in sin or do not spend time with God so when they get on stage, their singing lacks the anointing needed to bring down the glory of God.

iii. The church is not experiencing the glory of God these days because praise leaders do not *"come out of the holy place"* (2 Chr. 5:11). That is, stepping aside and handing the service over to the Holy Spirit. Most praise leaders/ music ministers lead the congregation to a point where God meets His people; however, they do not allow God to take over the service. You should not go on singing, talking, or even reading the scriptures, unless the Holy

Spirit leads you to do so, instead, allow God to fellow-ship with His people.

When you step aside, you make way for the Lord to *"...rise from His habitation"* (Zec. 2:13; Hab. 2:20) to strengthen His people (Isa. 40:31) through words of Prophecy, words of Knowledge and/or words of Wisdom (1 Cor. 14:3). God is always speaking to His people; however, our gathering offers a greater opportu-nity for Him to speak to us and for us to hear from Him; sometimes it is just a *'still small voice'* or that *'inner witness,'* which comes during the period of intense fel-lowship; that in my opinion, is all the people need for a particular challenge they are facing.

iv. A lot of praise leaders/music ministers have not learned to give all the glory to the Lord. After every powerful worship session, people will come to the minister to congratulate them for blessing them. Those accolades do not belong to the minister but God (Isa. 48:11). When we always give God all the glory, He will always show up when we gather.

v. There is often little or no harmony among the musicians. Whenever there is little coordination between the musi-cians and sometimes the media team in terms of distor-tions in the sound or the sound is too loud, it disrupts the move of the Spirit.

"12Also the Levites which were the singers, all of them of Asaph, of Heman, of Jeduthun, with their sons and their brethren, being arrayed

in white linen, having cymbals and psalteries and harps, stood at the east end of the altar, and with them an hundred and twenty priests sounding with trumpets:) [13]It came even to pass, as the TRUMPETERS AND SINGERS WERE AS ONE, TO MAKE ONE SOUND to be heard in praising and thanking the LORD; and when they lifted up their voice with the trumpets and cymbals and instruments of musick, and praised the LORD, saying, For he is good; for his mercy endureth for ever: that then the house was filled with a cloud, even the house of the LORD; [14]So that the priests could not stand to minister by reason of the cloud: for the glory of the LORD had filled the house of God." **2 Chronicles 5: 12-14**

The musicians arrayed in white linen, which represents personal sanctification; *'were as one,'* representing unity; and *'made one sound'* – in harmony and melodiously. Their message was singular; *"the Lord is good for his mercy endureth forever,"* meaning they had one purpose. The New Testament church is supposed to be *'the carrier of God's glory.'* Music ministers, let us aim at experiencing the glory of God every time we minister.

3. Learning and Teaching the Congregation New Songs

Another duty of music ministers is learning and teaching the congregation new songs. Every music minister must develop the habit of learning new songs regularly, as that makes the minister current and increases his/her stock of songs; Spirit-filled songs. I have found that one of the ways of recognizing the movement of the Spirit of God is through songs. The more songs you know; the easier it is to recognize the move of the Spirit. This is not to say the minister should abandon the Bible and prayer and think they can easily recognize the Spirit of God.

Learning new songs also contributes to church growth. Everybody likes to live in a peaceful and joyful environment. A church in which there is a lot of singing, love, and mer-rymaking, is certainly a peaceful and joyful church and will attract a lot of people. The members of the church will always look forward to another exciting time in God's presence week after week.

This is confirmed in Mike Murdock's book *"The Young Minister's Handbook"*, where he wrote that: *"one of the ways of keeping your ministry active is to learn new songs. The fast-est-growing churches in America are those who are learning new songs continuously: wherever there is fresh music, there seems to be fresh anointing."* [82] Jesus said, *"And I, if I am lifted up from the earth, will draw all men unto me"* (Joh. 12:32). Although this verse of scripture is referring to His crucifixion and resurrection, it is also applicable to praising Him. When we praise Jesus, we lift Him up.

A lot of church leaders wonder why their congregation is not growing. They might have done all the evangelism and follow-ups but to no avail. You had better check the legs upon which the church is standing; one, two, or all three of the legs may not be rightly fixed or positioned. In Acts 2:46-47, we

---

[82] (Murdock 1999)

are told that the apostle and the new converts continued "*daily with one accord in the temple, and breaking bread from house to house, did eat their meat with gladness and singleness of heart, **praising God**, and having favor with all the people. And the Lord added to the church daily such as should be saved.*"

Mr./Madam music minister do not stop learning and teaching your congregation new songs until the church gets to the level the Lord desires. Develop your skills to the highest level and project them to the glory of God.

4. Coordinating Music in the Church

Coordinating music in the local church is another duty of a music minister. The music minister works closely with the pastor to plan all the musical activities of the church. This is important because good music reinforces the pastor's sermon. There has to be a close collaboration between the pastor and the music minister. This explains why in most traditional churches the preacher for the day is usually the one who selects the hymns for service because the songs have to be in harmony with the message. If there is that close collaboration between the pastor and the music minister, the pastor can even tell the music minister the theme of his sermon so he can select the right songs.

The music minister should also work with the technical or media team to ensure that good music is produced at every service. This is because the spiritual needs of the congregation differ from service to service. That is the more reason why the Lord gives different messages for different seasons. When there is that close collaboration between the music and the technical teams, the Lord's desire for every service will be unhindered by human or technical errors.

The music minister is also in charge of selecting songs for service, leading or appointing persons to lead the praise for every service. Selecting songs for service sometimes appears to be very simple, but on the contrary, it is very laborious. The minister has to be spiritually in tune to discern the desire of the Spirit of God for every service. The minister should also know the congregation and the kind of songs they can handle. He/she should know the strengths of his/her co-ministers, as this may influence the songs they select for service. The music minister should also work closely with the Host to ensure the service runs smoothly.

In cases where the minister is also in charge of the choir, the work is even more laborious. He/she should have the skill to know the various parts and teach the choir to harmonize the songs at rehearsal before ministration. In this case, he/she needs to work closely with the various part leaders. This is the reason why I recommend only skillful and spiritually matured persons to lead music in church because it can be very frustrating at times.

5. Contribute to building the local Church

The minister of music should be actively involved in building the church. In most churches, the minister has oversight responsibility for a group of other musicians. The minister should be able to encourage members of the team to get involved in church activities, which will contribute to the overall growth of the church.

The music department is one of the departments that experiences a lot of attacks. As the leader or a member of the team, the minister should be able to stand in the gap and pray for the team regularly. By the office they occupy, the minister should become an automatic intercessor, otherwise, a lot of things will go wrong under his/her watch (see the chapter on the qualities of music ministers).

Their prayer should also cover the church, the leaders, and the various activities of the church. They must contribute their time, knowledge, and other resources to build a formidable team that will be an instrument of praise and honor to the Lord. The music minister should also be actively involved in pastoring his team. He should purposefully make disciples. The burden of feeding the flock (Act. 20:28-29, 1 Pet. 5:1-2) should not be laid only on the Lead pastor of the church, but every member, including the music minister.

Prayer

May the God of heaven help you to identify and understand what your duties are as a music minister so that you will fulfill His purpose for calling you, amen!

There are many examples of music ministers in the Bible, so in the next chapter, we will examine the lives of two great music ministers.

Chapter 7

The Great Music
Ministers of History

In this chapter, I have examined the lives of two music ministers: Lucifer in heaven and David on earth; their peculiarities, and the things that made them great.

1. Lucifer

The fourteenth chapter of the book of Isaiah contains prophecies about the restoration of the Jewish nation, the fall of the king of Babylon, the destruction of the Assyrian empire, and the ruins of Palestine. However, it also provides insights about a being named Lucifer. By all the accounts, he appears to have been an important being in the courts of God. He also appears to have been created with special abilities to make music; hence, I have described him as the first minister of music in heaven. The books of Isaiah and Ezekiel also give us insights into what led to his fall.

> *"How art thou fallen from heaven, O Lucifer,*
> *son of the morning! how art thou cut down to*
> *the ground, which didst weaken the nations!"*
> **Isaiah 14:12**

Lucifer was just not one of the angels, he was created to minister to God in music. Before he became "the Satan", he was called the son of the morning. According to Smith's Bible Dictionary, the name Lucifer means *"light-bearer or son of the morning."*[83] The Bible does not tell us the authority he had; however, it is believed he occupied a very honorable position. As the light-bearer, he bore the glory of God. He might have served as the special assistant to the Trinity because he stood in the presence of God. From the account in Isaiah, he could have even been second in command after the Trinity (Father, Son, and Holy Spirit). Lucifer might have been the closest to the throne of God than any other angel at that time.

According to Gill's exposition on the entire Bible, the name Lucifer *"alludes to the star Venus, which is the phosphorus or morning star that ushers in the light of the morning and shows that day is at hand." "This light speedily disappears before the far greater splendor of the sun."* [84] Lucifer is said to have been the usher of the morning light, which implies that his ministration ushered the light of God at the dawn of a new day, brought hope of a better day, a new beginning, and an opportunity to accomplish the things that could not be completed the previous day.

---

[83] (Smith 2016)

[84] (Gill 1809)

> *"Thou art the anointed cherub that covereth and I have set thee so..." Ezekiel 28:14*

Lucifer was also created as an anointed cherub that covers, which means that he was even closer than other heavenly beings. The book of Isaiah also gives us the names of two main groups of angels that are close to the throne of God; the seraphim and the cherubim.

> *"Above it stood the seraphim: each one had six wings; with twain, he covered his face, and with twain, he covered his feet, and with twain, he did fly." Isaiah 6:2*

The prophet Isaiah gives us some descriptions of the seraphim and their role in heaven. The word seraphim means *"the fiery or burning ones."* They appear in Isaiah 6:3 to repeatedly proclaim God's supreme holiness and glory, not directly to Him, but they call out to each other in God's presence. The seraphim's sole responsibility is to worship Adonai. The Smith Bible Dictionary says that *"their occupation was twofold; to celebrate the praises of Jehovah's holiness and power* (Isa. 6:3) *and to act as the medium of communication between heaven and earth"* [85] (Isa. 6:6). According to Isaiah, they worship God from above the throne, which is kind of vague in describing their closeness to the throne of God.

The seraphim have faces, feet, hands, and six wings. Two of the six wings are used to cover their faces, which symbolizes humility and reverence; the other two are used to cover their

---

[85] (Smith 2016)

feet, which is a symbol of respect; and the last pair of wings are used to fly, which is a sign of their readiness to do God's will. By covering their faces, the seraphim consider themselves unworthy to look upon the face of the Almighty God and also in obedience to God's warning that no one could see His face and live (Exo. 33:20).

In addition to worshipping God, the seraphim are also involved in the work of purification: *⁶ Then flew one of the seraphim unto me, having a live coal in his hand, which he had taken with the tongs from off the altar: ⁷ And he laid it upon my mouth, and said, Lo, this hath touched thy lips; and thine iniquity is taken away, and thy sin purged* (Isa. 6:6-7). To prepare Isaiah for his assignment, God sent one of the seraphim with a live coal in his hand, which he had taken with the tongs from the altar to cleanse Isaiah's sins by fire. Thank God, we do not need to be cleansed with fire from the altar because we have the blood of Christ.

The cherubim, the group Lucifer was a part of, on the other hand, are guardian angels. They have two wings, which, according to the Scriptures, are used to cover the glory of God that rests on the Mercy-Seat (Exo. 25:18). Those on the Ark had their wings stretched forth, one at each end of the Mercy-Seat and they faced *"towards each other and the Mercy-Seat."* The vision of Ezekiel also provides more description of these creatures:

> **"And every one had four faces: the first face was the face of a cherub, and the second face was the face of a man, and the third the face of a lion, and the fourth the face of an eagle."**
> **Ezekiel 10:14**

*"He bowed the heavens also and came down:
and darkness was under his feet. And he rode
upon a cherub, and did fly: yea, he did fly upon
the wings of the wind." Psalm 18:9-10*

Could the multi-face nature of Satan be an explanation for the reason why he can disguise himself as any creature he likes, and even possess animate and inanimate objects to use them for his diabolic agenda? Well, that is just my thoughts.

There is also an other group of beings called the *"living creatures"* in Revelation 4:6-7. They resemble the angels in Ezekiel and Isaiah, but they are full of eyes in front and behind them, and they function before and around the throne of God. One looks like a lion, the other, like a calf, and the third, like a man, and the fourth, like a flying eagle. Each of the creatures has six wings. *"They have no rest day and night, saying: Holy, holy, holy, is the Lord God, the Almighty, who was and who is and who is to come."* Could Lucifer have been part of this group of living creatures, as well? It is not very clear.

There was another group of beings the Bible refers to as sons of God. Job 38:7 says *"When the morning stars sang together, and all the sons of God shouted for joy...."* Job 1:6 also says: *"Now there was a day when the sons of God came to present themselves before the LORD, and Satan came also among them."* There were other sons of God, and it appears that Lucifer was part of that group, otherwise, he would not have had the permission to join their meeting. He might have had some authority over the other sons of the morning, or he was simply the first among his equals. For Lucifer to be *"the anointed cherub that covereth"* meant that he performed two roles: he covered, channeled, or directed the glory to God while worship took place, and he led the other angels to worship God. These roles align with some of the duties of music ministers described in chapter six, namely, creating the atmosphere for worship and leading others to do the same.

> *"... Thou sealest up the sum, full of wisdom, and perfect in beauty." "Thou wast upon the holy mountain of God; thou hast walked up and down in the midst of the stones of fire."*
> **Ezekiel 28:12, 14**

He did not only walk in the corridors of power, but he resided there, *"thou wast upon the holy mountain of God; thou hast walked up and down amid the stones of fire."* What qualified him to dwell on the mount of God? He was *"the anointed cherub that covereth."* God created and anointed him specifically for that purpose. There is no other creature at that time who was well-fashioned like him. Lucifer was clothed with excellence, an epitome of beauty. This tells us that whoever associates with God will be beautiful and wise. He was created and clothed to serve at the very source of the power that created everything.

> *"Thou hast been in Eden the garden of God; every precious stone was thy covering, the sardius, topaz, and the diamond, the beryl, the onyx, and the jasper, the sapphire, the emerald, and the carbuncle, and gold: the workmanship*

of thy tabrets and of thy pipes was prepared in
thee in the day that thou wast created."

Ezekiel 28:13

2. David

All through the Bible, the greatest music minister ever recorded was David. He was the initiator of the dynamic use of music in worship; the first person to establish a praise team. As a teenager, David lived a life of continuous praise to God while tending his father's herd of sheep in the hill country of Judah.

When he assumed the reign as king over the whole of Israel, he resolved to bring the Ark of the Covenant to his new capital, Jerusalem (2 Sam. 6). Until then it was the stronghold of the Jebusites (2 Sam. 5:7). He built a new Tabernacle in Jerusalem to house the Ark and went to bring the Ark from the house of Abinadab at Kirjath-jearim. On the way, there was a fatality that temporarily disrupted his plans but he learned his lessons and fulfilled his dream.

The Most Holy Place (the Holy of Holies) was the most important chamber within the old Tabernacle (the Tabernacle of Moses) because it housed the Ark of the Covenant. This represented the ever-dwelling Presence of God among His people. However, after the Ark was captured by the Philistines (1 Sam. 4:11), that chamber lost its significance in the Tabernacle of Moses. According to Psalm 78:6, it was the Lord who "*delivered his strength into captivity, and his glory into the enemy's hands*", the Philistines. About seventy years had gone by since the erection of the old Tabernacle at Shiloh. At the time David took over the reign of Israel, the old Tabernacle was situated at Gibeah, and Zadok, the Priest, was the one who supervised the daily sacrifices. The old order of worship still went on but without the most important article of all, the Ark of the Covenant.

When David finally had the opportunity to bring the Ark from the house of Obed-edom to Jerusalem, he placed the Ark in the new Tent he built. The Bible records how he brought the Ark of the Covenant into Jerusalem "*leaping and dancing*" (2 Sam. 6:16). Can you imagine the president of your country leaping and dancing on national television during a church service? That was what David did; he put aside his royal robes and insignia in that triumphant moment to wear a linen ephod. David knew the value of praising God and carefully set and arranged all the rituals of divine worship at Jerusalem and made Abiathar, the High Priest over the New Tabernacle. This was the beginning of a new religious era of spiritual and economic reform the nation had ever known. Singing songs of thanksgiving and praise was for the first time introduced into public worship and Mount Zion became "*God's holy hill*" (1 Chr. 16). This was a different kind of worship, where musical instruments of different kinds were used, and a large number of Levites praised the Lord continually. He put together a team of God-fearing and skillful Levites to make music to the Lord as they brought the Ark.

"So the Levites appointed Heman the son of Joel; and of his brethren, Asaph the son of Berechiah; and of the sons of Merari their brethren, Ethan the son of Kushaiah; So the

> *singers, Heman, Asaph, and Ethan, were*
> *appointed to sound with cymbals of brass."*
> **1 Chronicles 15:17, 19**

After the Ark of the Lord finally settled on Mount Zion, He maintained those Levites in the service of God. David chose 4,000 musicians out of the 38,000 Levites in the kingdom during his reign. About 288 of those musicians were skillfully trained to play music. They were divided into 24 teams, each of which consisted of a full band of 154 musicians, presided over by 12 specially trained leaders. They were under the leadership of one of the twenty-four sons of Asaph, Heman, and Jeduthun.

> *"David and the chiefs of the service also set*
> *apart for the service the sons of Asaph, and of*
> *Heman, and of Jeduthun, who prophesied with*
> *lyres, with harps, and with cymbals. The list*
> *of those who did the work and of their duties*
> *was: Of the sons of Asaph: Zaccur, Joseph,*
> *Nethaniah, and Asharelah, sons of Asaph,*
> *under the direction of Asaph, who prophesied*
> *under the direction of the king. Of Jeduthun,*
> *the sons of Jeduthun: Gedaliah, Zeri, Jeshaiah,*
> *Shimei, Hashabiah, and Mattithiah, six, under*
> *the direction of their father Jeduthun, who*
> *prophesied with the lyre in thanksgiving and*
> *praise to the LORD. Of Heman, the sons of*
> *Heman: Bukkiah, Mattaniah, Uzziel, Shebuel*
> *and Jerimoth, Hananiah, Hanani, Eliathah,*
> *Giddalti, and Romamti-ezer, Joshbekashah,*

Mallothi, Hothir, Mahazioth. All these were the sons of Heman the king's seer, according to the promise of God to exalt him, for God had given Heman fourteen sons and three daughters. They were all under the direction of their father in the music in the house of the LORD with cymbals, harps, and lyres for the service of the house of God. Asaph, Jeduthun, and Heman were under the order of the king. The number of them along with their brothers, who were trained in singing to the LORD, all who were skilful, was 288." **1 Chronicles 25:1-7**

Wow! An orchestra of 4,000 people doing nothing but singing praises to the Lord Jehovah continually! I do not know of any huge orchestra such as this anywhere in this world. Christian musicians, we need to take a cue from this and polish the gifts God has blessed us with. Get skilled, oh, talented musician, so you can give our King quality praise at all times.

I believe that the sound of music could be heard in Israel throughout the day.

The Bible is not clear on how each of these 24 teams functioned, but I believe each of the teams ministered for an hour a day. If there were 24 teams, then it presupposes that there was a different team praising the Lord throughout the day, at least for an hour. If this is true, then I believe that the sound of music could be heard in Israel throughout the day. Isn't that amazing? I am sure David had a revelation of heavenly worship, otherwise, he would not have authored such revolutionary praise.

Psalm 134:1 says: *"Behold, bless ye the LORD, all ye servants of the LORD, which by night stand in the house of the LORD."* This confirms the fact that some of the Levites made music to the Lord throughout the night. Indeed the Levites praised God 24 hours a day.

Each of the groups established by David had specific mandates. The sons of Asaph under his supervision ministered according to the order of the king. This implies the sons of Asaph ministered whenever the king wanted them to minister or when the king went to worship. The name Asaph in Hebrew means a *'collector'*.[86] He was a poet and musician and later established a school of poetry and musical composition.

Jeduthun and his sons also ministered with a harp and gave thanks and praise to the LORD. His team (his sons) played the cymbals. He was also the general overseer of music in the Temple. His name means *'laudatory or praising'*.[87] He is also called Ethan, which means *'enduring or permanent.*[88] Finally, Heman and his sons were the King's seers in the words of God and to lift up the horn of the Lord. The name Heman in Hebrew means *'faithful'*[89] and he was also a singer (1 Chr. 6:33; 16:41; 25:1).

> *Musicians, whether instrumentalists or vocalists should be collectors of people, faithful to their God and their local church, and their spirituality and skill should endure or stand the test of time.*

---

[86] (Strong 2009, # H623)

[87] (Strong 2009, # H3038)

[88] (Strong 2009, # H387)

[89] (Strong 2009, # H1968)

The meanings of the names of David's choir leaders are spiritually significant to us today. Musicians, whether instrumentalists or vocalists should be collectors of people. In other words, they should be lovely, soul winners, and easily approachable. Musicians should be faithful to their God and their local church. They may be celebrities, but that should not overshadow their faithfulness to God and the church. Finally, their spirituality and skill should endure or stand the test of time. In other words, they should be skillful and well-grounded in their faith.

Why did the Bible describe their duties as prophesying? Were these Levites prophets? These Levites were not necessarily prophets, but they spoke and sang prophetically; that is under the inspiration of the Holy Spirit. The psalms they composed and sang were prophetic, which talked about things to come and are still relevant and edifying to the church today. All these Levites joined in a special chant written and taught by David and other great servants of God. It is recorded that David even created some of the musical instruments that were used to worship the Lord.

> *"Moreover four thousand were porters, and four thousand praised the LORD with the instruments which I made, said David, to praise therewith."* **1 Chronicles 23:5**

David placed the Kohathites in charge of the Tabernacle. Kohath was the second of the three sons of Levi; Gershonites and the Merarites (Num. 3:17), from whom the three principal divisions of the Levites derived their origin and their name (Gen. 46:11; Exo. 6:16). During the period Israel wandered in the wilderness, the sons of Kohath (Kohathites) were in charge of the holiest portions in the Tabernacle, namely: *"the ark, the table, the candlestick, the altars, and the vessels of the sanctuary wherewith they minister, the screen, and all the service"* (Num. 3:31).

Solomon was neither a musician nor a music minister; but, under his father's instructions, he built the magnificent Temple and brought to fruition the desire of David to unite the Ark of the Covenant with *"all the things that David his father had dedicated; the silver, the gold, and all the instruments. ...out of the city of David, which is Zion"* (2 Chr. 5:1-2). At the dedication of the Temple, thousands of animals were sacrificed, alongside the singing of praises and we are told the glory of God filled the Temple mightily. When all righteousness is fulfilled, the glory of God will never be absent from our gathering because He delights in *"the praises of his people"* (Psa. 22:3).

3. You Can Become One Too!

You can be one of the greatest music ministers ever created; a person whose greatest desire is to praise God differently. After Lucifer was evicted from heaven, God reserved the music ministry for the church, His beloved bride. You are therefore privileged to be living in such an era and serving as a music minister. I thank God for making me part of the church; a generation the people of old desired to see. Although David did not live in the church age, he foresaw this era and lived within its shadows.

Jesus has given you all you need to succeed. You, therefore, do not have any excuse. You need to hold the office in high esteem and give yourself to learning to get to the height the Lord desires you to attain. Do not be content with what you have, go out there and trade with the talent and get more, so you can receive the Lord's reward for faithfulness (Mat. 25:14-30). Do your best to leave a mark and make a difference. Be the best you can be by achieving your potential through the ministry the Lord has placed you in.

> *"Therefore, since we are surrounded by so great a cloud of witnesses, let us also lay aside every weight, and sin which clings so closely, and let us run with endurance the race that is set before us, looking to Jesus, the founder and perfecter of our faith, who for the joy that was set before him endured the cross, despising the shame, and is seated at the right hand of the throne of God."* **Hebrews 12:1-2 ESV**

Please get rid of everything that can pull you down, whether they are sins, weights, or all other forms of mental strongholds. If you are not serious about your relationship with Jesus, get serious because He is waiting for you to do so. Develop a fresh desire for the Lord, seek him and you will find Him.

Prayer

Father, make me one of the greatest worshippers who has ever walked on the surface of this earth, in Jesus' name.

In the next chapter, I will turn our attention to some of the mistakes the great music ministers written about in this chapter made.

Chapter 8

The Pitfalls of Music Ministers

M usic ministers, like any minister in the church, are likely to make mistakes that can destroy their ministry. Songs of Solomon 2:15 says *"take us the foxes, the little foxes that spoil the vines; for our vines have tender grapes."* These pitfalls start in subtle ways; the very things you may overlook, over time they take roots, mature, and bear fruits. They become snares that trap the minister into all manner of sins. At that point, the minister finds it very difficult to overcome. It is therefore very important to identify these common mistakes music ministers are likely to make before they destroy them (Isa. 5:13; Hos. 4:6). They may not necessarily be sins but can become strongholds the devil can use to bring the minister down. We will study these pitfalls using the stories of Lucifer and David. The list of pitfalls provided here is not exhaustive, but I see them as the foundation of all other mistakes music ministers find themselves making.

1. The Pitfalls of Lucifer

"How art thou fallen from heaven, O Lucifer, son of the morning! How art thou cut down to the ground, which didst weaken the nations?"
Isaiah 14:12

The fourteenth chapter of the book of Isaiah outlines the mistakes Lucifer made when he occupied the heavenly office of a music minister. Those mistakes resulted in his downfall and his eventual dismissal from the high office. The above verse says he fell from heaven! The Hebrew word from which the word *"fell"* was translated is *"naphal."*[90] *Naphal* has a great variety of applications; however, the application used here is to *"lose an inheritance."*

Losing something may be through acts of omission or commission, however, Lucifer's loss was a deliberate act of commission. He wanted something that did not belong to him, so he lost what he had. It is good to be ambitious, but you cannot achieve anything without making sacrifices. The Holy Scriptures enjoins us to be content with what we have because it is great gain (1Tim. 6:6).

According to Barnes' notes on the Bible *"Lucifer's glory was dimmed; his brightness quenched."*[91] Unfortunately for Lucifer, the glory did not belong to him, it was a borrowed glory, and disconnecting from the source of glory meant, dimming the glory. Music ministers should bear in mind that their excellent ministrations are not good enough reason to think that

---

[90] (Strong 2009, # H5307)

[91] (Barnes 1845)

they are indispensable and without them, the glory of God will not descend. It is important to remember you are only an usher of the glory of God. When your work is done, please step aside and allow the Spirit of God to have His way.

Why did Lucifer attempt to usurp God's position? What made him think he could even achieve it anyway? Rev. Phiri in his sermon entitled *"Ambition for position"* (November 17, 2008), identified three reasons why Lucifer rebelled against God, namely: proximity, pride, and perceived injury. With his permission, I have discussed the pitfalls of Lucifer along these lines. Let us get right into them.

a. Proximity

Lucifer was one of the closest, if not the closest to Elohim among the angels in heaven at that time. His closeness to God meant he saw how God administered the entire universe. He did not only have access to the mountain of God, but he resided there. As Ezekiel 28:14 says: *"...thou wast upon the holy mountain of God; thou hast walked up and down in the midst of the stones of fire."* Lucifer walked in the corridors of power and therefore thought he could take over the helm of affairs. As a result, he started undermining the authority and power of God. What he forgot was that he was not the creator but a creation of God.

This is one of the pitfalls of music ministers and all who are in support ministries. The fact that you occupy a position of authority or because you are closer to leadership does not make you as powerful in terms of authority in that local church as the leader. You may be equally anointed or even be more

The fact that you occupy a position of authority or because you are closer to leadership does not make you as powerful in terms of authority in that local church as the leader.

experienced than your leader but that is not a license to overthrow Him (1 Sam. 24). I am not over-amplifying the office of leaders and making them untouchable in terms of positive criticism and correction. I am only calling for everyone to accord their leader the respect and honor due them. If you know you cannot serve under a particular leader, leave to where you know you can function comfortably. There is no need to openly challenge your leader. There is a ministry out there that you can comfortably fit in. This is, however, not a reason for leadership to treat their support staff anyhow or discriminate against them.

Some leaders also think that because they occupy the high office in the body of Christ, they are licensed to manhandle their support staff. Please remember that you are first and foremost, a Christian and then a leader; therefore, treat everybody Christ has redeemed with dignity. Your position of authority is a position of service and not to be served. When your focus shifts from serving to being served you will start manipulating, intimidating, and oppressing your flock. Whether you are the leader or support staff, we are supposed to work together and build the body of Christ. Each of us has roles to play, which we must keep performing until Christ returns for His church. Proximity in itself is not a sin so do not allow your proximity to leadership to cause you to sin. If you notice your proximity to leadership is breeding conflict and you have done all you can to resolve it to no avail, please withdraw and ask God for direction.

b. Pride

> *"...I will ascend into heaven, I will exalt my throne above the stars of God: I will sit also upon the mount of the congregation, in the sides of the north: I will ascend above the heights of the clouds; I will be like the most High..."* **Isaiah 14:13-15**

Pride was the second and most dangerous pitfall of Lucifer that led to his downfall. Unlike proximity, pride is a sin that God hates with a passion (Lev. 26:19; Pro.16:18; Isa. 16:6; 1 Pet. 5:5). Pride, as defined by the Webster's English Dictionary, is *"an inordinate self-esteem; an unreasonable conceit of one's own superiority in talents, beauty, wealth, accomplishments, rank or elevation in office, which manifests itself in lofty airs, distance, reserve, and often in contempt of others."* It can also be seen as *"insolence; rude treatment of others; insolent exultation."*[92] Pride is the foundation upon which the super-structure of rebellion stands. Like

> *Pride is "an inordinate self-esteem; an unreasonable conceit of one's own superiority in talents, beauty, wealth, accomplishments, rank or elevation in office, which manifests itself in lofty airs, distance, reserve, and often in contempt of others.*
> **Webster's English Dictionary**

---

[92] (Merriam-Webster 2011)

fuel, pride keeps the flame of sin burning (Pro. 16:18). Lucifer became so proud that he thought he could outwit his Creator. Within three verses he made references to himself five times: *"...I will..."* Can you imagine? It is amazing what pride can cause people to think about and do.

Someone who was once clad with so much splendor and majesty allowed the *"scales of pride"* to cover him (Job 41:15) to the extent of turning him into the *"king over all the children of pride"* (Job 41:34). I have witnessed how pride has destroyed the initial vision of ministries that had great prospects; how ambition and desire to have all members of the church bow to them have caused people to destroy the vision God gave them. Absolute power, they say *"corrupts absolutely"*, so those of us in authority should guide our ambitions and channel them to the glory of God, otherwise it will bring us down (Pro. 29:23).

God hates pride (Job 26:12; 1 Pet. 5:5) and He has put systems in place to bring down the proud (Isa. 23:9; Isa. 25:11; Jam. 4:6; 1 Pet. 5:5). What was the basis of Lucifer's pride? As we read from the definition of pride, it results from people's talent, beauty, wealth, accomplishments, and rank. These were the specific reasons why Lucifer became proud; his rank in heaven, his beauty, and his talent contributed. Let us examine each of these reasons separately and find out how they contributed to Lucifer's downfall.

i. His Rank

> *"Thou art the anointed cherub that covereth;*
> *and I have set thee so: thou wast upon the holy*

> *mountain of God; thou hast walked up and*
> *down in the midst of the stones of fire."*
> **Ezekiel 28:14**

In the first place, Lucifer was *"the anointed cherub that covereth."* He was the only angel in the Bible who was addressed by the title *"the anointed cherub."* Lucifer was very influential as evident in Revelation 12:3-4 which says: *"... behold a great red dragon, having seven heads and ten horns, and seven crowns upon his heads. And his tail drew the third part of the stars of heaven, and did cast them to the earth..."*

Lucifer performed the role of a guardian angel; covering and channeling the glory that emanated from the worship to God while worship took place. In addition, he was the chief worshipper; the leader of the choir.

The word translated as anointed is the Hebrew word *"mimshach"*,[93] which means to outspread, that is, with outstretched wings. The word also comes from another word *"mashach,"* which means *'to rub with oil to consecrate'*.[94] Lucifer was rubbed with oil and set apart to cover God's glory. He exercised some authority over a group of angels.

Mary Baxter in her book *"A Divine Revelation of Angels"* identified four ranks of the heavenly beings, namely: *"angels, archangels, Cherubim, and Seraphim."*[95] The Jewish daily lit-

---

[93] (Strong 2009, # H4473)

[94] (Strong 2009, # H4886)

[95] (Baxter 2003)

THE MUSIC MINISTER'S MANUAL

urgy also adds another set of angels called *Ophannim*[96] (living creatures) who constitute the heavenly choir together with the seraphim. According to Max Margolis, the *Ophannim* are *"the elect ministers of the Living God who are always ready to do the will of their maker with trembling, intone in sweet harmony the Thrice-holy."*[97]

As *"the anointed cherub that covereth,"* Lucifer performed the role of a guardian angel; covering and channeling the glory that emanated from the worship to God while worship took place. In addition, he was the chief worshipper, the leader of the choir. He, therefore, had access to the inner chamber of Elohim. It could be that Lucifer also had a place among the group of living creatures. Lucifer was a son of God (not the Son) because God had a lot of sons. It is clear from the scriptures that Lucifer was a member of the group of elite angels – the sons of the morning. Since sons have special places in their father's heart, he thought he could misbehave and get away with it. He wanted to take advantage of his position to topple Elohim.

> *"Now there was a day when the sons of God came to present themselves before the LORD, and Satan came also among them."* **Job 1:6**

> *"When the morning stars sang together, and all the sons of God shouted for joy?"* **Job 38:7**

---

[96] (McCracken 1978)

[97] (James et al. 1939)

Secondly, he was *"upon the holy mount of God"* and had access to the inner chamber of Elohim. The Hebrew word translated as *"was"* in the above scripture is *"Hayah"*,[98] which means *"to exist, that is, be or become, come to pass."* The Scriptures write of Gabriel as the one who *"...stands in the presence of God"* (Luk. 1:19), but Lucifer *dwelt* upon the holy mount of God. Every other angel entered and exited the mount of God, but Lucifer lived there. I am sure that he had certain privileges no other angel had. Thirdly, Lucifer walked up and down amid the stones of fire (seraphim). He had some prerogatives, the personal assistant of Elohim. He even heard the discussions of the Godhead; therefore, he thought he could use the secret of God against Him.

The best illustration of how privilege and prerogatives can make one proud that comes to mind is the position of the '*Krá*' of a Ghanaian traditional chief. The word *Krá* literally means the soul in Twi, a major language in Ghana. They are believed to be the souls of chiefs, their spiritual bodyguard against their enemies. If anybody attempts to kill the chief, the *Krá* will be the one to be affected. The *Krá* is usually a little boy or girl, and he or she sits in front of the chief as he rides head high in the palanquin during state functions. Such functions are usually accompanied by singing, drumming, and dancing, amidst much praise from the chief's subjects. The *Krá,* who also rides majestically in the palanquin hears and even receives some of the accolades the chief receives. It will be unthinkable and most disrespectful for the *Krá* to desire to usurp the authority of the chief simply because he or she rides in the same palanquin as the chief and receives the same level of praise as the chief. It

---

[98] (Strong 2009, # H1961)

will be tantamount to treason. This is not even possible because the *Krá* occupies that position because of the chief. He or she would not be in that position if that particular chief was not on the throne.

Similarly, Lucifer would not have been the son of the morning if Elohim had not made him so. Mr. music minister or Ms. lead vocalist, do not think because you can move the people when you minister or because you receive a lot of accolades after ministering, qualifies you to take the praise and glory that belongs to God (1 Chr. 16:29; Isa. 42:8). You are only a steward of the glory of God, therefore guard it with all diligence, and remember to give God all the glory. If you are in the support ministry and you start conceiving naughty ideas against your pastor, know that the spirit of Lucifer is not very far from you. God forbid that you should be an executor of Satan's agenda. May you never be the brain behind the split-up of any church of God. May you never become power drunk and be taken over by pride, in Jesus' name!

Lucifer was a prototype of every quality and virtue that anyone could desire; "full of wisdom, and perfect in beauty". He was a sight to behold, faultless and an epitome of beauty.

ii. His Beauty

The second basis of Lucifer's pride was his beauty. He was very attractive to look upon. You could not set eyes on him and not turn to look at him again. He was charming and handsome, a pleasant sight to behold. Lucifer had that bright radiance because Elohim made him so; God made him beautiful for His pleasure. Lucifer was a prototype of every quality and virtue that anyone could desire; *"full of wisdom, and perfect in beauty."* He was a sight to behold, faultless and an epitome of beauty. God decorated him with ten of the world's precious minerals. According to David Boshart article entitled *"Symbolism in the Bible,"*[99] the number ten speaks of government, which means Lucifer was a man of authority and under authority. Authority comes with special privileges such as grooming. God groomed Lucifer and made him gorgeous.

> *"[12]Son of man, take up a lamentation upon the king of Tyrus, and say unto him, Thus saith the Lord GOD; Thou sealest up the sum, full of wisdom, and perfect in beauty. [13]Thou hast been in Eden the garden of God; every precious stone was thy covering, the sardius, topaz, and the diamond, the beryl, the onyx, and the jasper, the sapphire, the emerald, and the carbuncle, and gold: the workmanship of thy tabrets and of thy pipes was prepared in thee in the day that thou wast created." "[17]Thine heart was lifted up because of thy beauty, thou hast corrupted thy wisdom by reason of thy brightness: I will cast thee to the ground, I will lay thee before kings, that they may behold thee."*
>
> **Ezekiel 28:12-13, 17**

The color combination of the precious stones covering Lucifer was stunning. The colors ranged from bright red

---

[99] (Boshart 2006)

(*sardius*); to a pale-green to a bottle-green and golden yellow or green (*Topaz*); to crystal (*diamond*); and from light green or bluish-green (*Beryl*); to white and reddish grey (*onyx*). The other colors included: light crystal (*jasper*), indigo blue (*sapphire*), glowing live coal (*emerald*), dark-red glowing coal (*carbuncle*), and bright yellow (*gold*). All the above precious stones are very hard, brilliant, and durable.

Do you know that almost all these precious stones were on the high priest's breastplate (Exo. 28:27) and formed part of the foundation of the New Jerusalem described in Revelation 21:20? Revelation 4 also mentions that these stones cover the "*One who sits on the throne*," meaning God clothed Lucifer with the same ornaments that covered Him, glory. When the light of God's glory shone on the stones, Lucifer glowed with beauty.

Lucifer served at the very source of the earth's beauty, so he thought he had it all. Similarly, the mantle that comes with all the offices within the Body of Christ, including the music ministry, comes with glory and beauty (Exo. 28:2, 40). However, beauty without character, the Bible says, '*is vain*' (Pro. 31:30). Lucifer's beauty got into his head and caused him to stop thinking straight. It is often said that beautiful people are usually very arrogant. With their beauty, they easily get what they want, manipulating people and systems in their favor. If this goes on unchecked, such people start seeing themselves as gods. That was the mistake of Lucifer!

The music ministry will make you beautiful (Psa. 33:1). Since God inhabits the praise of His people (Psa. 22:3); His glory will always be with you if you make Christ your righteousness. The ministry will bring you money and fame, which will enable you to buy whatever you need to look good. However, do not let the clothes, make-ups, and accolades affect your character. Be the sweet person you have always been and remain connected to your source of inspiration and glory – Jesus.

iii. His Talent

The third and final basis of Lucifer's pride was his Talent. According to Webster's English Dictionary, talent is a *"natural gift or endowment, skill or/and eminent ability."*[100] Lucifer had it all; talk of skill, natural endowments, and abilities. God endowed him with all there was to desire, to enable Lucifer to carry out His pleasure. According to Ezekiel the prophet: *"... the workmanship of thy tabrets and thy pipes was prepared in thee in the day that thou wast created"* (28:13).

God purposely made Lucifer what he was. God made no mistake in depositing all that skill and talent in him and fashioned the entire array of musical instruments into him for His purpose. He might have been the conductor of the heavenly orchestra. The little knowledge I have about the conductors of orchestras is that they should have been a lead instrumentalist of, at least, one of the parts. Usually, some conductors play more than five instruments very well. Going by the above descriptions: *"...the workmanship of thy tabrets and thy pipes,"* meant Lucifer could play all the musical instruments used to praise the Lord in heaven. In him was the summation of all the musical instruments used around the world, from the Americas to Africa, Asia, Europe, and Australia. That is the handiwork of God!

---

[100] (Merriam-Webster 2011)

I can imagine this anointed cherub standing about 9.7 feet tall; beautiful with his hair and wings well-groomed, beaming with the light of God's glory. As he raises his hands, I can hear the sound of different string instruments, brass, organs, and percussion instruments; some of the instruments I have never seen in my lifetime and the sounds I have never heard. I can hear the sound of different rhythms, melodies, and harmonies that earth has never produced in its entire existence; sounds that are incomprehensible to humans. In the process, the heavenly hosts also quickly take their positions of worship and praise to the Lord. I can hear the sound of music as he gracefully takes up his position on the mount of God. Even his steps produced the sounds of pipes, timberlines, and horns. This is incredible! He was just remarkable! Yet he was God's creation; one of His masterpieces.

Lucifer thought by detaching himself from God, he could function normally. That was not and will never be possible. How talented and skillful are you, O music minister, for which you are puffed-up? Mr./Ms. music minister, remember that whatever talent and skill you have belongs to God and you are only privileged to possess it. You cannot decide not to refuel your automobile and think it can travel every time without any problem. Without Jesus, we can do nothing (Joh. 15:5). A lot of people hold the notion that the gifts and calling of God are irrevocable (Rom. 11:29) so they can do anything with it and not be affected. They forget that the anointing supporting the gift and calling is revocable.

Rev. Phiri in his book *"Equipped for Ministry"* stated that: *"to be mightily used of God, your character must be bigger than your gift and not the other way round.*"[101] Do not allow your head to get swollen by the accolades, they belong to God, and He reserves the right to demand His talent anytime He wishes. Our Lord Jesus was different; He is Lord but emptied Himself of all the glory, honor, and power He had in heaven to carry out the purposes of God (Phil. 2:6-11). Christ's humility is the example we need to follow if we want to live to fulfill God's assignment for our lives.

c. Perceived Injury

The third and final pitfall of Lucifer is what Rev. Phiri termed *'perceived injury*, which simply means getting offended, angry, hurt, or displeased by the actions, attitudes, or words of someone in authority. Perceived Injury occurs when there is an unresolved offense, hurt, or when someone is disrespecting, abusing, or taking advantage of you. Jesus told the disciples *"It is impossible but that offenses will come: but woe unto him, through whom they come!"* (Luk. 17:1). When those hurtful feelings, resentments, and anger that begin as minor irritations or annoyances are not resolved, they degenerate into grievous sins. It is believed that it was a practice in heaven that whenever the angels gave glory, praise, and honor to God (Rev. 4:8-11), His glory glowed in intensity (Exo. 15:11) and Lucifer, who was a member of the sons of the morning, was supposed to prostrate in worship (Rev. 4:8-11). As he prostrated, the glory bounced on Lucifer's covering of precious stones and reflected to God.

[101] (Phiri 2008)

149

Lucifer was offended by the fact that he always had to give the glory back to God during worship.

I suspect that Lucifer was offended by the fact that he always had to give the glory back to God during worship. Remember, he was covered with the same gemstones that covered the throne of God, as such, he may have glowed like God Himself. He did not understand why he could not keep that glory and praise to himself but had to give it to God. I am sure that as he performed his worship duties, he used to dream of the day when he would be seated on God's throne and all the other creatures will bow to him. He forgot that God shares His glory with no one (Isa. 42:8). He did not know that God created Him and placed all those precious stones on him for His glory. His duty demanded that he gave glory to God whenever the Lord glowed in praise. He, therefore, fixed his eyes on the throne of God when he said: "...*I will be like the most High*" (Isa. 14:15).

Whenever you find yourself disliking something a pastor or church elder does, find out whether that feeling stems from your proximity, pride, and/or perceived injury, and deal with it. It is good to always deal with problems at their early stages before it degenerates into something satanic. A lot of the breakaways in churches today are a result of offenses. When people in the support ministry, including music ministers, begin to outperform their leaders, it tends to create friction between them and leadership. In such situations, it is better to sit together and solve the problem. If not resolved, it may degenerate into confrontations and quarrels, eventually leading to a breakaway. I am not entirely ruling out the nasty behaviors of some of our spiritual leaders, however, that is not a ticket to oppose what

God is doing in that ministry. If you try using dialogue to settle displeasure and nothing seems to be changing, leave.

Let me share another story relating to this topic of perceived injury or offense with you. I became friends with a young man back in high school because we were in the same house. At a point, I saw him more like a brother than a friend because I had lost my biological brother about a decade earlier. I shared a lot of my struggles with him, and we took counsel together. We later went to the same university and he went to medical school after the second year, as that was the procedure for students in the biological sciences, and I stayed on to complete my 4-year Bachelor of Arts degree. By design, the medical school was located in the same suburb I lived in at that time, so I visited him whenever I was home on holiday. We always discussed things related to church and the ministry, and over time, we worked together with him to start a church. Some other wonderful young men and women bought into the vision and, together, we worked hard to build the church.

I took on the role of raising a praise team and the choir because that was my ministry. I was still actively serving in my church, so my Sundays were very busy; I attended the first service at my church then leave for his church immediately afterward. Things caught on very well. After a little over a year, I got married and an opportunity opened for me to travel to Europe to do my masters. While doing my masters, we communicated regularly, and he encouraged me to return and continue my work in the choir. Upon completing my master's degree, I went to the UK to work for a year; save up, and purchased a few things to take back home to support his church.

I grew up knowing that the church was a place where everyone was welcomed and could contribute their resources in building the body of Christ, so I was eager to bring the knowledge and experience I'd gained in Europe to help grow my friend's church. I did not even visit my home church when I returned to Ghana. I felt we understood each other and could work together even better. But I was wrong, things were completely different; my friend had graduated from medical school, gotten married, and above all, had been ordained as a Rev Minister. My friend created an air of importance around himself. He was no longer approachable; even the way he walked changed and he spoke authoritatively to everyone around him. He called elders' meetings arbitrarily, which went on for hours without any clear agenda. It was unsettling for me because my first son was still under 2 years and staying for that long at church was unsettling. Worse of all, the teachings that were coming from the pulpit changed. They were spiteful and vengeful; the pulpit became the place to settle personal scores and say things that he would otherwise not be said to people personally. You could feel a sense of insecurity around him. Again, with his authority, he started interfering in the relationship of some of the young people in the church, breaking some and re-arranging others.

Initially, I could talk to him about some of the things I sensed were not right in a lovely way, but at a point, he stopped granting me that opportunity. Anytime that I requested to talk to him, he found an excuse for me. At some point, my friend no longer picked my calls in the name of waiting upon God. He never returned my calls either. The change in our relationship began to seriously trouble me. I could no longer bear it and felt it was time to move on. It took me months to make my decision, all the while, I tried to speak to my friend, but he never granted me an audience. When all attempts failed, I stepped down from my role in the choir and after a few weeks, I stopped attending church. After about two weeks, my friend never called to find out why my family was absent from church. I even became the topic of some of his sermons. I was seriously hurt by his behavior because I saw him as a brother. I thank God that I had learned how to handle offenses from Bible school and that also helped me to gracefully exit the church without causing any trouble and taking anyone out with me, but my family. Not long after I left the church, I had a dream that confirmed that my separation from my friend's church was the right decision.

As Jesus said (paraphrasing), you will get offended by people because they are as imperfect as you are, but the manner you handle the situation will determine whether you will glorify God or do the devil's bidding. I genuinely loved my friend and wanted to contribute to the work God was doing in his ministry, but it just did not work out. I just thank God that I did not cause any breakaway with my separation because I had a lot of influence there. When you are offended and you feel it cannot be resolved, leave, but don't take any of the church members with you, as the devil did in heaven, taking one-third of the angels with him. Many other families and individuals left after I did but I had nothing to do with it.

Let us now discuss some of King David's pitfalls, the sweet psalmist of Israel.

2. The Pitfalls of David

As already mentioned in chapter seven, David was one of the greatest music ministers of all time. Among the many things he did, the most fascinating of all, in my opinion, was the 4000-man orchestra that he built with the sole purpose of praising the Lord continually. Before this orchestra was developed, he committed an error that caused the life of someone and could have marred his plans, had he not learned from his mistake. My discussion is based on the story of David's attempt to move the Ark of God to Jerusalem, where he planned to be the center of worship. I have likened the moving of the Ark of God to the welcoming of God's presence during our corporate worship.

> *"⁴And all the congregation said that they would do so: for the thing was right in the eyes of all the people. ⁵So David gathered all Israel together, from Shihor of Egypt even unto the entering of Hemath, to bring the ark of God from Kirjathjearim. ⁶And David went up, and all Israel, to Baalah, that is, to Kirjathjearim, which belonged to Judah, to bring up thence the ark of God the LORD, that dwelleth between the cherubims, whose name is called on it. ⁷And they carried the ark of God in a new cart out of the house of Abinadab: and Uzza and Ahio drave the cart. ⁸And David and all Israel played before God with all their might, and with singing, and with harps, and with psalteries, and with timbrels, and with cymbals,*

*and with trumpets. ⁹And when they came unto
the threshingfloor of Chidon, Uzza put forth
his hand to hold the ark; for the oxen stum-
bled."* **1 Chronicles 13:4-9**

Below are a few errors I have identified from this passage
of scripture.

a. Failure to Enquire from God

David's failure to enquire from God or consult the Lord
before setting out on the mission of bringing the Ark of the
Covenant into Jerusalem (1 Sam. 23:2, 4, 11; 2 Sam. 2:1; 2 Sam.
5:19, 23), was his first mistake. He should have enquired from
the Lord as to whether it was the right time and how to move
the Ark. The Bible says: *"¹To everything there is a season and
a time to every purpose under the heaven. ¹¹He hath made
everything beautiful in his time: also he hath set the world in
their heart so that no man can find out the work that God
maketh from the beginning to the end"* (Ecc. 3:1, 11). He might
have received the revelation that it was the season to move the
Ark of Testimony back to its dwelling place, but it might have
not been the actual time. He should have waited for direction
before moving it. The Lord wanted him to continue to
rely on Him.

You may have great plans for your
ministry and want to do *'exploits'* for
the Lord. However, as music ministers, we need to cultivate the habit
of waiting on God before taking any

*Our failure to wait upon
God has contributed
to the increasing
dryness the church is
experiencing.*

155

decision concerning our ministry. Isaiah 40:31 says: "*But they that wait upon the LORD shall renew their strength; they shall mount up with wings as eagles; they shall run, and not be weary, and they shall walk, and not faint.*" Our failure to wait upon God has contributed to the increasing dryness the church is experiencing. When we wait on the Lord, we do not just get direction, we also get the strength to accomplish the task. Sometimes, even while ministering, the Lord will want us to take a certain action, so we need to constantly be in tune with the Holy Spirit until the work is done.

b. Failure to follow Protocol

The second major mistake David made was his failure to follow the approved way of moving the Ark of the Covenant. For the sake of clarity, I have subdivided this error into three different parts; lack of attention to detail, failure to use the right people, and failure to use the right mode of transportation.

i. Lack of Attention to Detail

Zeal alone is not enough to help ministers do the right things for the Kingdom of God, knowledge, and character are equally important.

After David "*smote the Jebusites and conquered their city,*" He thought it was a good idea to build "*a new tent to house the Ark of the Covenant*" (2 Sam. 5). He, therefore, went to bring the Ark from the house of Abinadab at Kirjathjearim, but he did not follow the laid-down rule of moving the Ark of Covenant. The Ark was

Israel's source of security and pride (2 Kin. 19:14-15, Psa. 80:1) and represented their well-being and success, strength and defense, provision, and protection. The absence of the Ark of Testimony from the city signified the absence of all the afore-mentioned benefits. The dwelling place of the Ark was a place of meeting, communion, and instruction (Exo. 25:22).

David's mission of restoring the Ark of God to its dwelling place was right. David even had the right attitude because the Scripture says: "*And David and all Israel played before God with all their might, and with singing, and with harps, and with psalteries, and with timbrels, and with cymbals, and with trumpet.*"

He was young and zealous; he had just been sworn in as king over a unified Israel and wanted to make the people happy. He also loved the Lord and wanted to put things in order, one of which was making Jehovah the God of Israel. However, in his zeal and excitement, David made serious mistakes that led to a fatality. Things were not done properly. He just did not read in-between the lines. Zeal alone is not enough to help ministers do the right things for the Kingdom of God, knowledge, and character are equally important. This is what Paul said about the zeal of Israel that made them think they were doing the right thing: "*For I bear them record that they have a zeal of God, but not according to knowledge*" (Rom. 10:2). Many young music ministers have been shipwrecked by their zeal because they did not pay a little attention to details or thought did not matter.

Such people have done unimaginable things that were avoidable if they had just enquired from God, waited a little bit more, or sought a second opinion. Do not ever get to a point and think to yourself: '*I have arrived*'; that will only give the devil the chance to get you. There is a protocol to follow when ministering to God and His people. Although it is not written out in *'black and white'*, we need to be in constant fellowship with the Spirit of God to discover it.

ii. Failure to use the Right People

David chose men from his army (1 Chr. 13:1). These men were warriors, men who had blood on their hands because of their numerous battles (2 Sam. 5: 17-25). The psalmist says: *"³Who shall ascend into the hill of the LORD? or who shall stand in his holy place? ⁴He that hath clean hands, and a pure heart; who hath not lifted his soul unto vanity, nor sworn deceitfully"* (Psa. 24:3-4). Clean hands represent our relationship with our fellow humans, while pure hearts speak of our relationship with God. These men had spilled a lot of blood, something God frowned on. If David wanted to involve them, he should have told them to at least, sanctify themselves.

God is not just looking for anybody to minister before Him, rather He wants those who have sanctified themselves.

Sometimes church leaders allow almost anybody to minister in music, especially, when the church is young, and the music department is not fully formed. However, that is a mistake because God is not just looking for anybody to minister before Him, rather He wants those who have sanctified themselves. Music ministers should learn to sanctify themselves before ministering. This will guarantee the presence of God at every ministration. Again, we are told that David *"gathered all Israel"* to accompany the Ark (1 Chr. 13:1), but that was not what the law commanded. The Ark of the Covenant was only supposed to be moved by the Levites, not *"all Israel"*. Fortunately for us, the only requirement we need to fulfill is to live for God through Jesus Christ.

iii. Failure to use the Right Mode of Transport

The other mistake David made was his mode of transporting the Ark of the Covenant. The Bible says: *"And they carried the ark of God in a new cart out of the house of Abinadab: and Uzza and Ahio drave the cart."* That was the greatest mistake of all! The Book of the law required that only the Priests and the Levites were supposed to come close to the Ark of God and minister before it (Num. 4:5, 6, 20; 1 Kin. 8:4). The Kohathites were specifically instructed to bear the Ark of God on their shoulders (Num. 4:15; 7:9; Jos. 6:4), but David and all Israel *"...carried the ark of God in a new cart... and Ahio drave the cart"* (1 Chr. 13:7).

The Ark represented the presence of God, and it is supposed to be carried by humans and not animals or inanimate objects. Therefore, transporting the presence of God on a new cart was wrong. That attracted the anger of God leading to the death of Uzziah. According to Strong, Ahio means *"brotherly"*,[102] but God was not looking for just anybody 'brotherly' to transport His Presence but someone who had been sanctified. His father Abinadab, who lived in Gibeah (the Benjamite quarter of Kirjath-jearim), was a Levite, which means Ahio was a Levite. It was required that as a Levite, Ahio was supposed to sanctify himself before bearing the Ark of God. There is no record that

---

[102] (Strong 2009, # H277)

159

Uzzah and Ahio sanctified themselves before accompanying the Ark of God.

As mentioned, the Kohathites were the people chosen and properly trained to bear the presence of God (Num. 3:31; Num. 4:15); they were the people with the right heart and attitudes toward God. People sanctified by God, not people who necessarily had good voices, were talented on the instrument, or those who can dance or shout the most. There was also a laid down pattern the procession of the Ark had to follow (Num. 10), but none of it was followed. There may not be any written procedure to follow in bringing down the presence of God, but that is a very good reason to rely on God for direction.

Where did David get this idea of transporting the Ark of God on a new cart from? From the Philistines, the Bible says: *"⁷Now, therefore, make a new cart, and take two milch kine, on which there hath come no yoke, and tie the kine to the cart, and bring their calves home from them: ⁸And take the ark of the LORD, and lay it upon the cart; and put the jewels of gold, which ye return him for a trespass offering, in a coffer by the side thereof; and send it away, that it may go"* (1 Sam. 6:7-8). The Philistines used the new cart because they were scared of what the God of Israel had done to them and did not know how best to get the Ark of God back to its place of origin. David and Israel, on the other hand, did not have an excuse for transporting the Ark on a cart. Israel was the custodian of the blueprint about worshipping God; thus they had no excuse.

This is a clear example of copying blindly from unbelievers. It is not always wrong to learn from unbelievers, but then when it comes to things related to worshiping God, it is an absolute 'No'; we need to be very careful. Mr./Ms. music minister do not take secular songs and add them to the church's repertoire *Mr./Ms. music minister do not take secular songs and add them to the church's repertoire because I am not sure God will be pleased with those kinds of songs.*
because I am not sure God will be pleased with those kinds of songs. We should not be the people hindering the move of God in our local church because we do not want to be the source of anyone's offense (Luk. 17:1-2; 1 Cor. 8.). As Christians, we need to rely on God to teach us His ways, we do not have to import the practices and culture of the world into the church in the name of modernization. God is the same yesterday, today and forever (Heb. 13:8), if He wants us to bring secularism into the church, He will tell us Himself.

It took David three months to learn how to move the Presence to Zion. Even throughout his time of learning and preparation, His attitude towards praising God did not change. Eventually, he and the entire nation brought the Ark with *"leaping and dancing before the LORD."* Thank God, David learned his lesson and did the right thing after the first mistake. He told the Levites and High Priest to sanctify themselves and carried the Ark of God on their shoulders.

"¹And David made him houses in the city of David, and prepared a place for the ark of God, and pitched for it a tent. ²Then David

said, None ought to carry the ark of God but the Levites: for them hath the LORD chosen to carry the ark of God and to minister unto him forever. ³And David gathered all Israel together to Jerusalem, to bring up the ark of the LORD unto his place, which he had prepared for it. ⁴And David assembled the children of Aaron, and the Levites... ¹¹And David called for Zadok and Abiathar the priests, and for the Levites, for Uriel, Asaiah, and Joel, Shemaiah, and Eliel, and Amminadab, ¹²And said unto them, Ye are the chief of the fathers of the Levites: SANCTIFY YOURSELVES, BOTH YE AND YOUR BRETHREN, THAT YE MAY BRING UP THE ARK OF THE LORD GOD OF ISRAEL UNTO THE PLACE THAT I HAVE PREPARED FOR IT. ¹³FOR BECAUSE YE DID IT NOT AT THE FIRST, THE LORD OUR GOD MADE A BREACH UPON US, FOR THAT, WE SOUGHT HIM NOT AFTER THE DUE ORDER. ¹⁴So the priests and the Levites sanctified themselves to bring up the ark of the LORD God of Israel. ¹⁵And the children of THE LEVITES BARE THE ARK OF GOD UPON THEIR SHOULDERS with the staves thereon, as Moses commanded according to the word of the LORD. ¹⁶And David spake to the chief of the Levites to appoint their brethren to be the singers with instruments of musick, psalteries

*and harps, and cymbals, sounding, by lifting up
the voice with joy." 1 Chronicles 15:1-4, 11-16*

David's heart was focused on worshiping God. It is no wonder God punished Saul's daughter, Michal for criticizing David for dancing like a commoner when the Ark of God was finally brought to Jerusalem.

Prayer

God help me not to fall victim to any of the pitfalls mentioned here so that my ministration will be pleasing to You, amen.

This concludes the first part of this book. In the second part, I have looked at some practical tips that will guide music ministers before, during, and after leading your local church to praise God.

Part II

"Preparation, the Music Minister's Secret"

Chapter 9

Keys to a Successful Ministration

1. Preparing to Minister

G ood preparation before ministration is of the essence as it guarantees the growth and success of the minister. The minister serves God through singing and communicates His love to the congregation. He also helps the congregation to better fellowship and serve God. Just as a preacher prepares; studying the Bible, praying, fasting, and seeking direction from God to prepare his/her sermon before a worship service, the music minister must prepare adequately before ministering.

In this chapter, I have shared some tips that can guide music ministers in their preparation for ministration. They may appear elementary, but they are the very things the minister needs to prepare and get the congregation ready for such a sacred time as praise and worship. What should the minister do in readiness for a time of fellowship with God? The minister should pray, plan and practice if they want to be successful at creating the right atmosphere for the congregation to meet and have fellowship with Jesus.

a. **Prayer**

So much goes into preparing to minister; however, prayer is the first and most important activity to consider and engage in. It is communicating with and hearing from God. It is the minister's connection to heaven and heaven's connection to the minister, so this channel should always be kept open. Without prayer, the minister will burn out and lose interest in the ministry easily.

The minister needs to pray about everything related to his/her impending ministration; about the day itself, the songs they will sing, the congregation, and for the leadership of the local church. The minister needs to ask the Lord to make him/her useful to Him throughout the impending ministration, ask for wisdom and guidance in how to love and lead His people according to His will, to help him/her cultivate a humble and teachable heart. The minister should also pray and hand over the service and the music team to the Lord. Supplications should also be made for the music team – your fellow ministers in the music department, that God will help you foster unity and cohesion during ministration.

Praying towards ministration alone is not sufficient, it should be linked to the minister's worship. The minister's worship is the foundation for a fruitful life and ministry (Psa. 27:4-8). According to Andrew Murray, "*many Christians look upon prayer as a burden and a duty; a difficulty to get alone with God.*"[103] When our prayer does not flow out of a heart of

---

[103] (Murray 1998)

worship, it becomes a burden. When we learn to be alone with God, he will prolong our ministry. If your prayer life is only connected to the periods you are ministering, you will not have a relationship with the Lord. The minister needs to remain connected to God!

Living a life of worship is also very important, that is, living a life that is pleasing and acceptable to the Lord, a life He can boast of (Job 1:8; Job 2:3). The life of worship should not begin on Sunday morning and end on Sunday evening; it ought to be a daily activity. The Father is not seeking Sunday worshippers but those who worship Him *"in spirit and in truth"* (Joh. 4:23-24), year in and year out. God intends that worship be a life-long process (Rom. 12:1), since *"in Him, we live and move and have our being"* (Act. 17:28). Remember that singing or playing the instrument is all about giving God our best and heartfelt worship. As ministers, guiding the people into God's presence is both an inexplicable joy and a great responsibility that should not be taken lightly. Learn to spend quality time with God, be sensitive to His prompting, and listen to Him when preparing to minister.

Guiding the people into His presence is both an inexplicable joy and a great responsibility that should not be taken lightly. Learn to spend quality time with God, be sensitive to His prompting, and listen to Him when preparing to minister.

Living a life of worship also includes having daily and regular personal devotions (prayer, fasting, Bible study, and meditation). This is the devotion you have alone with the Lord in your closet. This is the time you get to commune with the Lord and get personal instructions from Him concerning your life and ministry. God wants our worship to be living and our living worship; you need to be a friend of God. You cannot take others to a place you have not been or take them along a path you have never walked. You need to have something to share with the people and that comes by walking on the path of holiness. It is easy to differentiate the ministration of a minister who spends time with the Lord from the minister who does not. The former ministers under the unction of the Holy Spirit and the people get blessed. Living a life of worship also helps the minister discern the ways and works of the Lord (Psa. 103:7).

Often, music ministers concentrate only on developing their relationship with God and forget they need to have a good relationship with the people they lead (Rom. 12:18; 1 Joh. 4:20). Although it is important to have a good relationship with the Lord, it is equally important to have a good relationship with the congregation (Heb. 12:14). Never think you will succeed if you are not in the right standing with the people you lead. When you are not at peace with people, it can even affect your relationship with God. A good prayer and devotional life enhance the minister's relationship with people. Virtues such as honesty, integrity, love, and the like (Phil. 4:8), should be part of you. These virtues come by allowing the Holy Spirit to work on you daily and change you into the likeness of Christ (Gal. 5:22-23; Eph. 5:8-10).

b. Plan

Planning is the second most important activity after praying and living a life of worship. To build a healthy, strong, and growing ministry, the minister must be a good planner. Table

1 provides a simple plan that can guide the minister in his/her preparation.

Failing to plan will affect your ministry and in the long term, destroy it. A good plan will help the minister spend adequate time to wait on the Lord for direction and avoid picking songs that are not relevant for the day. All activities leading to the ministration on Sunday ought to be planned. Most ministers set a day or two aside to plan, however, it is important to set aside a few minutes every day during the week to prepare.

Table 1: A sample guide for preparing towards ministration

Day	Time (as suitable)	Activity
Monday	30 minutes	• Pray about the impending ministration. • Prepare your repertoire.
Tuesday	20 to 30 minutes	• Find the keys, arrange, and rehearse the selected songs
Wednesday	30 minutes	• Pray over the songs and make necessary changes. • Send songs to musicians.
Thursday	30 minutes	• Take and review feedbacks from team members. • Make final corrections.
Friday	20 minutes	• Send the songs to the media team leader and music team members.
Saturday	1 to 2 hours	• Rehearse with the team.

Sunday	15 to 30 minutes	• Be at the church premises to ensure everything is ready and pray as a team before the service starts. • Pray immediately after service. • Evaluate the day's ministration. • Start preparing for the next ministration and rehearse.

c. Develop a Repertoire

To develop a repertoire for ministration, the minister must identify the purpose of the service or the theme. The minister needs to identify the session he/she is leading. You need to ask yourself questions such as: am I leading praise and adoration or am I leading the choir to minister? What type of songs will be needed for the occasion? Are the content Biblical? Are the lyrics of the songs doctrinally sound? Do the songs arouse spiritual thought? Do they inspire the congregation to seek God? Are they excellent? Do the songs fit the need of the congregation? Do the songs produce a wholesome response? Does the musical style or the composers' name draw people to godliness?[104]

By asking these questions, the minister will have a good basis to develop his/her repertoire. Asking yourself the above questions will enable you to avoid making traditions or personal preferences priority over the will of God (1 Cor. 4:6) when selecting your songs. There is much value in selected

---

[104] (Erb 2009)

singing by choirs or special groups provided the focus on such singing is not on entertainment but true expressions of worship, so select your songs with care. For example, if you are leading praise and adoration, the songs list should include songs of thanksgiving, praise, and adoration.

Remember that songs of praise, thanksgiving, and adoration are meant to please God and not men. This knowledge should guide you when selecting your songs. If you are leading the choir to minister to the congregation, select songs that will exhort, comfort, and motivate your audience. This is how Paul the apostle puts it: "...*Let all things be done for edification*" (1 Cor. 14:26). A well-developed repertoire will build up the church through edification, without giving offense or causing anybody to stumble (Rom. 14:7-21).

The congregation's ability to handle complex songs and varied musical tastes must also be considered. The minister must be cautious when employing different styles in the service so that the song will be within the acceptance levels of everyone; both the young and old, the rich and poor, educated and the uneducated. It is sometimes good to have some hymns in your repertoire to cater to those who like them. Remember, you need not use worldly music in worship because it can cause a spiritual offset. The most appropriate music for worship is the one that draws your brother or sister towards the Lord and away from "*this present evil age*" (Gal. 1:4). The beauty of any worship service lies in the simplicity of the activities; this includes the songs that are sung.

The average person in the congregation should be given songs they can easily sing during worship. The melody, key signature, range of notes, tempo, and arrangement should be within their ability to handle so they can fully participate in the service. It is good to group songs of the same key together to facilitate the smooth transition between your worship songs. This makes sense on a musical level; however, it may not always work on a vocal level. So, take note of this when selecting your songs. According to Cheong *"unless you have very good musicians, pick simple keys such as C Major, A Minor, D Major, G Major, E Minor, and A Major."*[105] In cases where all the songs selected do not have the same key signature; there should be breaks between the songs. This break can be filled with a brief moment of prayer, Scripture reading, or words of praise.

God also uses the right songs, sung with the right heart to visit and fellowship with His people. Therefore, the minister needs to prayerfully select their songs, and keep praying over them until they are used in ministration. In prayer, God will tell you how He feels about the songs you have selected. When the right repertoire is composed, the Lord will guide you to fulfill His purpose for the day by showing you the order in which the songs need to be arranged and sung. Sometimes, He even shows you the particular songs on your list He will need and when He will have you sing them during the service. At times, God will direct you to use only one or two songs in your repertoire, no matter its style, tempo, or key.

Building your repertoire prayerfully will enable you to meet the spiritual needs of the congregation as well. When you regularly pray over your song list, there will be a lot of variety in your songs, which will meet the needs of every member of the congregation. This time of prayer will make you more sensitive to the Lord. That is when He also gives you specific messages

---

[105] (Cheong 1999)

for the congregation. This may take the form of a portion of scripture, a word of knowledge, a word of wisdom, or a word of prophecy.

Finally, although it is good to prepare for ministration; you should always remember to create room for God to move among His people. You must be ready to listen to God throughout your ministration. You should not overdo things during that period. Just create the atmosphere for God and step aside.

c. Practice

After carefully developing your repertoire, you need to rehearse the songs before ministering them. The best illustration that comes to mind is cooking and serving your meal. You cannot spend all the time cooking your meal and serving them without tasting them; you need to savor your meal before serving it to others. Practicing the songs on your own before using them will help you personalize the songs by making the lyrics, content, or message of the songs clear. No matter how busy you are, make time for a personal rehearsal. It does not matter whether you are familiar with the songs or not, just make time for rehearsals.

Rehearsing your songs will help you review your repertoire and make any necessary changes (such as the song choices, the arrangements, the key, etc.) before submitting it to the media team. It also helps you prepare properly before rehearsing with the entire team. Rehearsing your songs is a way of honoring God as that shows Him your level of commitment to giving Him your best. Practicing is important in your skill development as a minister. Depending on your skill, it is estimated that on average, a team needs about 2 rehearsals of about 1 to 2 hours each week to prepare for a 40-minute session. A one-man team only needs 45 minutes at most to rehearse for worship. In our fast-paced societies and lives, an hour and a half of practice time may be the best you can get. So, make time on your own to rehearse your songs.

Practicing also means memorizing the lyrics of the songs. Unlike the traditional hymns that are lengthy and difficult to memorize, contemporary praise and adoration music is simple and easy to memorize. Why memorize the lyrics if you can sing from the music sheet or the projected words on the screen? When you memorize the lyrics, you free yourself to be more expressive with the song. Secondly, you can concentrate on the worship and work at reaching the peak of the service, where God ministers to the congregation on an individual level.

Make sure you sleep early the day before you lead worship. The night before is not ideal for staying up late watching movies or the like. When you do, it may have an upsetting effect on your preparedness. You need to be relaxed and show no sign of fatigue or stress. Dress decently on the day of ministration. Do not make any room for the devil to tempt you or any member of the congregation by what you wear to minister. On the day of ministration, you have to get to the premises at least 15 minutes before the service begins to pray together as a team. It is also the best time to warm up your voices.

2. Stage Performance

The second important ingredient to a successful ministration is your stage performance. I have followed the ministry of prominent local and international music ministers, and I can say with confidence that their performance on stage contributes immensely to their success. The following are to be noted about your performance:

It is very important to know about the stage on which you will be ministering, particularly if it is a stage, you are not familiar with. Knowing about the stage will help you plan and manage your movements. For example, very little movement will be required if the stage area is small. If it is a large stage, then you can move across the stage. Again, a solid stage, rough or slippery will help you know what to wear to the stage.

When mounting the stage, you need to walk briskly with confidence and enthusiasm. Do not show any sign of arrogance or fear. If you know the key you will be ministering in, quickly inform the musicians before you raise any song. It is even advisable to give the instrumentalist a copy of your repertoire before you mount the stage. This information is particularly useful for praise leaders. If you are mounting the stage as a team, file on stage orderly and take your position. Do not talk on stage and try to order the arrangement of your colleagues, leave that to the music director. Do not get on stage and try doing your make-up.

Make sure you wear a smile and establish eye contact with the congregation. Be very mindful of your movements and gestures on stage. Make sure you utilize the entire stage but stay at a certain section for a while before moving on to the next, particularly when you are the lead vocalist. You should also know how far or quickly you can move because most of our services are streamed live these days. This will prevent your performance from looking haphazard or rushed. When you pick up the microphone, you can check whether it is turned on by simply talking into it. Do not strike the top of the microphone as it may damage the diaphragm. Handle the microphone well to get the best output.

Do not let the microphone obstruct your face but try to keep it roughly 2 inches down and away from your mouth when singing softer sections of your song. You however need to pull it further away from your mouth when projecting your voice at the climax of your ministration. When the microphone does not obstruct your face, it helps you maintain excellent eye contact with the congregation. It also prevents saliva from entering the microphone, which can reduce the lifespan of the microphone. Again, it will help the media team get a better view of your face if your ministration is being captured on video or camera. Do not fidget with the microphone while talking or singing since it may produce an irritating sound that will distract the people.

Do not directly point the microphone towards the speakers or the monitor on stage as it will cause serious feedback and, in some cases, even damage the sound system. As much as possible, do not fold the microphone cable because it may lead to breakages, rather let it hang loosely. Only fold the microphone cable when it will help keep the microphone connected to the cable. Thankfully, there are more cordless microphones these days.

Do not carry your worries, bitterness, anger, or any kind of negative emotions on stage. Emotions are very contagious, thus, when you carry a negative emotion on stage, you may end up transferring that spirit to the congregation or hinder the move of the Spirit of God. The congregation may also misinterpret the meaning of your negative emotion. A stony face on stage can be very discouraging. Keep a smiling face no matter how fired-up or down you are. Stand relaxed but in a friendly posture. Avoid projecting a lack of direction and purpose.

3. When Ministering

The time for ministration varies from congregation to congregation, however, in most churches, it comes immediately after the opening prayer or the time of intercession. In cases where it does not come immediately after the time of prayer, the people may not be in the mood for praises, therefore it will be necessary to get them into the mood by using phrases that will get them into a meditative mood and stop talking to one another.

Opening with a short exhortation is another excellent way of getting the congregation into the mood to worship. The word exhortation means to encourage, embolden, cheer, and advise. It prepares members of the congregation who were not present for prayer for the time of praise and adoration. Exhortation helps the congregation get to your level of preparedness before leading them into the presence of God. If this is not done, you will struggle during your ministration.

The exhortation should be based on the word of God and not your thoughts. Your experiences can be used to support the word of God but that should not be the main focus. If you truly wait on God, He will give you a message for His people. More often than not, the exhortation is always in line with the day's sermon because there will always be a central theme running through the prayer, the exhortation, the praise songs, and the sermon if the leaders of the various sessions wait on the Lord.

Be economical with your words as exhortations are not sermons. A maximum of two minutes of exhortation should suffice. If your exhortation exceeds three minutes the message will be lost. The Bible says *"Guard your steps when you go to the house of God and be more ready to hear than to give the sacrifice of fools... Do not be rash with your mouth, and do not let your heart be hasty to say a word before God. For God is in Heaven, and you are on earth; therefore let your words be few"* (Ecc 5:1-2).

The time of exhortation is not the time to show off the number of Scriptures you can quote, how knowledgeable you are, or how spiritual you are. It is simply the time to prepare the congregation to meet with God. It is not the time to read long portions of the Bible but about giving the people a message; a reason to sing praises to God. Before you start singing give the congregation some time to meditate upon what you have shared with them. This will help them internalize the message you have shared with them and help them to worship.

You can continue by leading them to pray and thank God for His goodness. When you start singing, sing thanksgiving, praise, and adoration songs (Psa. 92:1; Psa. 100:4a). The type of songs, whether they are thanksgiving, praise, or adoration, do not refer to the tempo of the songs as it is erroneously known; rather it refers to the lyrics or the words of the songs. Depending on the time allotted for praises, you need to proportionally divide the time to cover the entire range of songs prepared for worship. Note, you do not necessarily have to sing all the songs on your repertoire, but you only have to be sensitive to the Spirit of God. He may want you to sing only a few of the songs on your repertoire, which will be just what you need for that day. Sometimes the minister may have to skip some songs while repeating others because the unction of God may be strong on those songs, and they need not be changed until the Spirit completes His work; bringing the congregation closer to God.

One very important session in our services that is usually overlooked is the period of silence. We have put God on the listening side of our relationship with Him and all we do is to talk, bark and shout at Him, giving Him very little opportunity to speak to us individually. However, every true relationship can be described as *two-way traffic.*' True Biblical worship includes moments of silence and listening. It is as important as auditory music and words. This is the most relevant, yet the most difficult period to accomplish for the amateur music minister. They can easily miss it or overlook it because their level of sensitivity may not be highly developed. Every leader needs to be sensitive to the Spirit of God to be able to discern God's readiness to fellowship with His people. In other words, the music minister should be able to identify the voice of God (see the next chapter).

Silence and listening are the climaxes of the worship; the period the leader 'steps aside or comes out' (1 Kings 8:10-11) to allow God to take charge (Habakkuk 2:20) of the service.

Why is the period of silence and listening very important in worship? Silence and listening are the climaxes of the worship; the period the leader '*steps aside or comes out*' (1 King. 8:10-11) to allow God to take charge (Hab. 2:20) of the service. This is not a period for supplication but a period to respond to the manifestation of God's majesty and awe. It is the period we express our deepest love and adoration for the Lord. The period of silence and listening takes the worshiper out of time into God's eternity. It is a period of inexplicable experience and absolute peace and fulfillment. When we wait on God in silence, we relinquish control to God, which enables us to freely listen to Him.

That is the period where the revelation gifts operate. The period of silence may last from a few seconds to about 10 minutes. It is therefore advisable to sing slow-tempo songs to ensure a smooth transition into the period of silence. I prefer to sing slow-tempo songs at the beginning of the praise and adoration session to get ample time to peak and step aside for God to take control. When the session is properly observed, there will be an atmosphere of total peace and joy in the auditorium.

Some reasons why the period of silence is not observed in churches include:

a. Most Church leaders do not know its importance in worship.
b. Music ministers may not know how to go about observing it.
c. There may be too many activities on the program for worship that day; and
d. The music minister did not allocate enough time to that session when he/she was planning for ministration.

4. After Ministering

Lead the congregation to thank God for His visitation before you get off the stage. Never forget to give God all the glory because it belongs to Him (Isa. 42:8; 48:11). At the end of the service, you should first meet as a team to pray and thank God and give Him all the glory before doing any other thing.

It is good to start preparing immediately for the next ministration whether you know when it will be or not. Why wait until the next session when you have all the time to do so. What do you do between one ministration and the other? Rev. Dr. Phiri wrote that *"prayer is not like a spare tire; you cannot just leave it in your trunk and expect it to be effective when you need it. You must be persistent in your prayers."* In other words, stay in constant touch with God. You need to continue living a life of worship. God wants your worship to transcend the boundaries of Sunday to a daily activity targeted at pleasing Him and keeping yourself from every form of evil.

Just as Paul told the Thessalonians, I say the music minister must *"Abstain from all appearance of evil"* (1 The. 5:22), such as: *"...all malice, and all guile, and hypocrisies, and envies, and all evil speaking"* (1 Pet. 2:1). Live at peace with everyone. Confess your sins as soon as you commit them and settle every problem you have with people so that nothing will mar your relationship with the Lord. I will end this chapter by joining John the apostle to say:

> *"²Beloved, now are we the sons of God, and it doth not yet appear what we shall be: but we know that, when he shall appear, we shall be like him; for we shall see him as he is. ³And every man that hath this hope in him purifieth himself, even as he is pure."* **1 John 3:2-3**

Prayer

Father, help us practice all that we have learned to enable us to be the kind of ministers that will bring You the utmost glory, in Jesus' name.

In the next chapter, we will study the ways we can identify the voice of God, before, during, and after ministering.

Chapter 10

Developing Sensitivity to the Voice of God

Many voices operate in this world; the voice of Satan (Gen. 3:1, 4, 5; Job 1:7-12 and 2:1-6; Mat. 4:1-13.) and his demons (Luk. 4:33-34; Act. 8:7); the voice of men (Act. 5:29); the voice of the flesh (Jon. 4:8; Luk. 16:3, 18:4; Jer. 10:23), as well as the voice of God (Joh. 10:3-5, 14, 16, 27), which is the safest and most secured voice to follow. A music minister's ability to distinguish between the voice of God and the many other voices is one of the most important abilities he/she can have. Every day, life presents different situations in which ministers need to make choices that will determine whether or not they will do the perfect will of God. It is very necessary to hear the voice of God in every situation to understand His will (Eph. 5:17) and take the right decision. Our ability to hear the voice of God in a particular situation is ever more critical in these times where information is being generated at a supersonic speed.

THE MUSIC MINISTER'S MANUAL

> *"I am the good shepherd, and know my sheep,*
> *and am known of mine. My sheep hear my*
> *voice, and I know them, and they follow me."*
> **John 10:14, 27**

> *"But strong meat belongeth to them that are of*
> *full age, even those who by reason of use have*
> *their senses exercised to discern both good and*
> *evil."* **Hebrews 5:14**

God desires to speak to us more than we would ever long to hear from him, in reality, He is always speaking, yet we do not hear Him because we are often not listening. The book of Job says, *"for God speaks again and again, though people do not recognize it"* (Job 33:14 NLT). The Bible is an expression of His longing to reveal himself to you. There are 66 books, 1,189 chapters, 31,205 verses, and over 2,500 promises in the Bible. A cursory search of the phrases: *"… and the Lord said…"*, *"…saith the Lord…"*, *"…He said…"* and *"…God said…"* in the Bible showed that they occur 163, 815, 470, and 46 times respectively. Adding the number of times all these phrases are cited comes up to 1,494 times. If these are the number of times God spoke to the nation of Israel about major events, can you imagine how much He is saying to the over 7 billion people living today? I cannot even fathom the number of thoughts He has for me (Isa. 55:8-10)!

The average woman and man use about 20,000 and 7,000 words respectively in a day.[106] If these are the number of times the average man and woman speak in the day, which is just with

---

[106] (Hammond 2013)

a few 10s of people, can you imagine how much God is saying to all His children around the world every second? God is very interested in everything His children do, and He is willing to guide us if only we will listen. God wants to have a relationship with us; He actually created us for fellowship with Him. When we decide to draw close to God, His voice becomes more and more clear to us. Learning to receive divine guidance is therefore very important to every Christian, especially, to music ministers. We need to learn to walk in intimate fellowship with God if we want to receive divine guidance in every area of our lives. You cannot live anyhow and expect to be able to recognize the voice of God with ease.

How God Speaks

There are only two major ways by which God speaks to His children: namely, by the written word and by other means. The authenticity of the other means is based on the written word of God. The word of God is the only infallible medium humans can rely on.

1. Primary Way

God speaks to mankind through His written Word, the "*Logos*".[107] The written word of God is the only true and reliable source of the voice of God (2 Tim. 3:16). It is the final authority when it comes to receiving instructions from God (Rom. 15:4). God does not speak concerning things already revealed in His Word and He will also not say anything contrary to His written

---

[107] (Strong 2009, # G3056)

> *God does not speak concerning things already revealed in His Word and He will also not say anything contrary to His written Word. Even when He uses other means of communication, they will never conflict with His written Word.*

Word. Even when He uses other means of communication, they will never conflict with His written Word. As music ministers, God expects us to know His Word. You need to *"study to shew thyself approved unto God, a workman that needeth not to be ashamed…"* (2 Tim. 2:15). To test the other voices you hear, you need to know His Word (1 The. 5:21).

Another aspect of the written word is what is known as *"Rhema"* in Greek.[108] This refers to the living or life-giving word of God. In other words, it is the written word coming alive in an individual's situation. It applies to a specific situation, meets a personal need, and provides individual guidance. As to what *"Rhema"* you will receive in a situation depends on how much *"Logos"* you know, your availability, your level of sensitivity, and how the Holy Spirit wishes to communicate that word to you.

Your ability to recognize the Word as it applies to a specific need or situation in your life makes it a life-giving Word to you. A *"Rhema"* may be communicated through a sermon, an exhortation, or a verse from the Bible which suddenly comes alive to you with great meaning. It is usually received with the help of the Holy Spirit. It may also be spoken in your inner spirit by the Lord. You will get to learn more about the inner witness later in this chapter. The *"Rhema"* will always agree with the

---

[108] (Strong 2009, # G4487)

"*Logos.*" The verses below speak of the relationship between the "*Logos*" and the "*Rhema*":

> **"He that rejecteth me, and receiveth, not my words (Rhema), hath one that judgeth him: the word (logos) that I have spoken, the same shall judge him in the last day." John 12:48**

> **"[18]For ye are not come unto the mount that might be touched, and that burned with fire, nor unto blackness, and darkness, and tempest, [19]And the sound of a trumpet, and the voice of words (Rhema); which voice they that heard intreated that the word (logos) should not be spoken to them anymore." Hebrews 12:18 -19**

2. Secondary Ways God Speaks

The secondary ways God speaks to His children are also very important. Graham Fitzpatrick in his book "*How to recognize God's Voice*",[109] outlined two other means through which God speaks to His children. According to him, there are situations in every individual's life the Bible does not give a specific answer. Again, advances in technology have complicated life's situations. These secondary ways are:

---

[109] (Fitzpatrick 1984)

a. **Internal sources**

i. The inner witness of God the Holy Spirit.

ii. The "still small voice" or inner voice of God the Holy Spirit.

iii. Dreams.

iv. Visions.

b. **External sources**

i. Signs in our circumstances.

ii. Audible voice.

iii. Angelic visitation.

iv. Human sources: sermons, exhortations, prophecies, words of wisdom, and words of knowledge and counseling.

For the sake of the office of the music minister and the kind of ministration he/she offers, I will dwell on the inner witness of God the Holy Spirit, the *'still small voice'* and signs in our circumstances. These are quick and easy ways God speaks to music ministers while preparing for ministration and while in the line of duty. I would like to reiterate that, the written word of God is the only standard by which we can test whether the source of an incoming message is of God.

i. The Inner Witness of God; the Holy Spirit

"The Spirit itself beareth witness with our spirit, that we are the children of God." **Romans 8:16**

The Inner Witness is an inner conviction or spiritual sensation that reveals the mind of God for a situation you are in. It comes in the form of intense peace (Phil. 4:7) and joy, or a lack of joy and a horrible uneasy and tight feeling in your spirit when you are praying and/or thinking about making a decision.[110] It is not a physical feeling or emotion, but a spiritual awareness. Have you ever felt *"checked"* in your spirit when you were about to do something? That is the inner witness and God's way of trying to get your attention. His promise is, *"I will make you wise...show you where to go...and watch over you"* (Psa. 32:8 NCV). This sensation cannot be explained, you just know it. Obeying this sensation often results in doing the will of God, overcoming temptation, or escaping from an accident. This inner witness should always be checked against the word of God before obeying it because the Holy Scriptures are the only authentic source of spiritual guidance.

According to Rev. Dr. Phiri in his daily devotional (December 20, 2010) *"Our lack of peace was the Holy Spirit calling 'time out'...We don't know the future, God does, and He directs our steps by the way of peace, or lack of it. The Holy Spirit acts as a referee. When the players stay within the boundaries, they are free to move about. But when there's trouble, or the ball goes out of bounds, the referee blows the whistle, stops play, and restores order."*

Our feelings are the voice of the body, deeply seated in the flesh. The flesh is an enemy of the spirit (Rom. 8:7-8; Gal. 5:17). Feelings are deceptive so God does not use your feelings to speak to you. Reasoning, on the other hand, is the voice of the mind, situated in your soul. God's ways are often beyond

---

[110] (Fitzpatrick 1984)

human reasoning, so He does not use our reason to speak to us. Again, God's thought processes are much higher than ours (Isa. 55:9). 1 Corinthians 2:14 says *"But the natural man receiveth, not the things of the Spirit of God: for they are foolishness unto him: neither can he know them because they are spiritually discerned."* You need to be on the same spiritual frequency to discern the voice of God.

Finally, conscience is the voice of the spirit of man, convicting and directing us to the perfect will of God. The Holy Spirit speaks to our spirit and the spirit convicts the conscience. Through this process, you are brought into conformity with the will of God. When the Holy Spirit speaks to your spirit, the conscience is convicted, but if you continually ignore it, your conscience will get to a point where it will be *"seared"* (1 Tim. 4:2). At this point, your spirit becomes hardened to the conviction of the Holy Spirit, and you get led by your flesh.

As music ministers, we should aim at developing our spirit and conscience to the point where it can easily intercept the inner witness of the Holy Spirit. As already mentioned, there are certain situations in life that the written word does not say anything about, therefore the music minister has to depend on his/her inner witness to know the will of God for that situation. For example, the Bible does not tell you the kind of songs you need to sing for a particular day's service, neither does it tell you at what point during your ministration you have to stop singing and let the people keep quiet, so you need to depend on the inner witness to guide you.

I know you are asking: how can I develop this inner witness? I have already answered this question, but it is worth mentioning again. The inner witness is developed by cultivating an intimate relationship with the Lord (Joh. 10:27). Spending time with Him alone in fellowship; not petitioning Him but just fellowshipping with Him. The inner witness is one of the powerful secondary ways God speaks to me when I am ministering, and I have seen the great manifestation of His power by simply obeying the instructions given.

ii. **The Still Small Voice or Inner Voice of God**

> *"And after the earthquake a fire; but the LORD was not in the fire: and after the fire a still small voice."* **1 Kings 19:12**

The still small voice, or what other translation renders as the "*soft whisper*" (HCSB) is not audible to the human ear. It is a spiritual thought God places in the human mind through his spirit. These thoughts come in the form of words and often result in mental pictures of what God is telling you.[111] When God wants to say something very important to His children, He often uses the still small voice just below the absolute threshold of hearing (ATH). Whisper is employed for the sake of secrecy and intimacy.

When God wants to say something very important to His children, He often uses the still small voice just below the absolute threshold of hearing (ATH). Whisper is employed for the sake of secrecy and intimacy.

---

[111] (Fitzpatrick 1984)

**"If you wander off the road to the right or the
left, you will hear his voice behind you saying,
"Here is the road. Follow it. Isaiah 30:21 GNB**

The above scripture is an example of how God guides His
people using the still small voice. It is often heard behind you,
kind of intrusive; but it aims at instructing you in righteousness. Yeah, it speaks to our conscience and leads us to do the
things God approves of. Like the inner witness, obeying the
promptings of the still small voice results in doing the will of
God, overcoming temptation, or escaping from an accident. In
the situation presented by the scripture above, the people were
led to abandon their idols to follow the commands of God.
According to Mark Batterson, *"the relational, emotional, and
spiritual problems"* we face *"are actually hearing problems
– ears that have been deafened to the voice of God; it's that
inability to hear His voice that causes us to lose our voice and
lose our way. If you are not willing to listen to everything God
has to say, you eventually won't hear anything He has to say."*
[112] You often hear people saying *"...and something told me..."*,
that could be the still small voice, but we need to be careful not
to assume that every voice we hear is from God because the
devil can impersonate the still small voice. Always test what
you hear against the word of God. I have escaped many traps
of the enemy by simply acting upon the promptings I received
by the still small voice.

Let me share one of the instances God spoke to me using
the still small voice that saved my daughter from being run over
by a vehicle. I was going to get a few things from the grocery

---

[112] (Batterson 2017)

shop and she ask to go with me. When we exited our apartment building to the parking lot, she had to go pick her sweater because it was a bit cold. I told her to meet me at the garage, which was across, on the other side of the parking lot. Upon reaching the garage, I just saw a picture of my daughter running out of the building onto the driveway without stopping to look before crossing the driveway. As soon as I saw that picture, I returned and stood at the entrance to wait for her. Truly, when she exited the building, she run directly onto the driveway. Just then a van drove to where I was standing. Thankfully, I was there to grab her before she ran onto the driveway. If I had not obeyed the still small voice and returned to wait for her, the story would have been different. Thank God for the mental pictures He gave me.

Why does God speak to us in whispers rather than in audible voices? Mark Batterson answers this question perfectly. According to him, God whispers *"softer and softer so that we can get closer and closer to hear His heart."* He added that when we *"finally get close enough, He envelops us in His arms and tells us that He loves us."* [113] Jesus said something to Nicodemus when He was speaking to him about being born again, which I think provides some insight to why God speaks to His children in whispers; He said *"The wind bloweth where it listeth, and thou hearest the sound thereof, **but canst not tell whence it cometh, and whither it goeth**: so is every one that is born of the Spirit"*(Joh. 3:8). I also think God whispers to conceal His instructions and our obedience to those instructions from the enemy. Like I had already mentioned, God loves us and wants the best for us, hence He will do everything to

---

[113] (Batterson 2017)

lead us into His perfect will, that is, if only we are willing and available.

iii. Signs In Our Circumstances

God also communicates to His children through circumstances. Although circumstances are usually beyond your control, they do not occur outside the knowledge of God. Even when they are perceived to be out of His will, God is still in control and uses those unpleasant circumstances to fulfill His purposes. One excellent example in the Bible is the Old Testament story of Joseph (Gen. 37-50). Joseph's brothers sold him into slavery in Egypt simply because of their jealousy, yet with time Joseph understood how God used their jealousy to serve His purpose for not just Joseph's family but the lives of multitudes.

Sometimes the unpleasant nature of the circumstance may not allow us to believe God has a hand in it, but believe me, God always works with it

> *"⁵Now, therefore, be not grieved, nor angry with yourselves that ye sold me hither; for God did send me before you to preserve life...⁷And God sent me before you to preserve you a posterity in the earth and to save your lives by a great deliverance. ⁸So now it was not you that sent me hither, but God."* **Genesis 45:5, 7-8**

God used Joseph to save the lives of thousands of people in a time of severe famine by using an unpleasant circumstance.

If God had used a more pleasant situation to get Joseph into Egypt, things may have not worked out the way God intended and Joseph may have not learned that important lesson of his life. A similar example took place in the life of Paul. He wanted to visit the Thessalonians but was hindered by Satan (1 Thes. 2:18). As a result of his inability to visit them, he wrote to them, and this is how we got first and second Thessalonians. Paul's seemingly unfortunate circumstance produced this powerful book that had and continues to have a greater impact than his visit would have had. This epistle has been passed down through the centuries for the benefit of all believers. Sometimes the unpleasant nature of the circumstance may not allow us to believe God has a hand in it, but believe me, God always works with it. We should always find the purpose of God for the situation or circumstance.

Going back to the story I shared earlier about our praise festival when I was pursuing my undergraduate studies, the circumstances at that time meant that we could not have a full hour of praise because the ES wanted to have a communion service. We could have just thrown our hands in the air and produced a mediocre festival. Since I was very sensitive to the voice of

When you encounter an unfortunate circumstance, you need to look at it in the light of God's word. Ask yourself whether the outcome of the circumstance will make you better in your relationship with God.

God at that time, He used the circumstance to draw me deeper in intimacy with Him. God also showed His glory and did something that had never happened in MPU. I can say with absolute confidence that most of the things I have written in this book were learned when I thought the odds were against my ministry. When you encounter an unfortunate circumstance, you need to look at it in the light of God's word. Ask yourself whether the outcome of the circumstance will make you better in your relationship with God. Always view the circumstances of your life in the light of what God has revealed in His written word.

Let me segue into another story of how God used an unpleasant situation to communicate His purpose for my ministry. I decided to enroll in a Bible college at a point in my life because it had always been my dream to go to bible school. I seriously wanted to know more about the scriptures from an academic point of view. A few months into the program, the dean of the college, who served as an associate Pastor in one of the local churches in town, asked my class, during one of our lectures, that His church needed a musician to support their praise team because the church's organist had traveled out of town and would not be back for a couple of months. I was learning to play the acoustic guitar at that time, so I told him that I could play the guitar, however, I would have to speak to my wife about our transition to their church. He said that was a great idea. I saw that as an opportunity to play to improve my skills because better guitarists were playing in the church I was attending at the time, and I did not get the opportunity to play there. My wife did not like the idea but after some convincing, she agreed, and we transitioned into our new church.

A few months after we joined the church, the pianist returned, and our ministrations got even better. The church was small, so having the full house all the time was a challenge. Gradually, we started losing our vocalists because of work transfers and other personal commitments. Some days, during our rehearsals, there were more instrumentalists than vocalists, and on other days, there were no vocalists at all. In those cases, the pianist had to play and sing at the same time. It was becoming very tiring for him, so during one of our rehearsals, I volunteered to lead worship for the first time on one Sunday. My ministration went well, but after the service, the senior pastor announced that she wanted to meet the worship team.

To my total surprise, rather than complimenting us for doing our best in that situation, she scolded us. The pastor went something like "God has called everyone into an office, and He expects us to remain and function in that office." The pastor added, "If God has called you as an instrumentalist, stay in your lane, do not make yourself a singer and vice versa." The pastor went on and on ranting for about 10 minutes, we were all surprised and we just sat there motionless and said nothing. I was so disappointed because this pastor did not know me that well; the pastor had no clue as to what my calling was, she just assumed that I was a guitarist because I could play, I was actually a vocalist at that time and was just learning to play.

Not long after that, the cycle of absenteeism started again, for weeks there were no vocalists and the pianist had to play and lead praise and worship every Sunday. After ministering for a while, the pianist asked me to prepare to lead the following Sunday. I quickly remarked, "do you want Pastor to scold us again?" We both just laughed about it and we carried on with our rehearsal. At church the following day, the pianist's request for me to lead praise was weighing heavily on my mind throughout church service that day. I was torn between going by want the pastor said and doing what I know I was called to do. As I thought about the situation, the story I shared earlier about our worship festival came to mind. That was a sign that God wanted me to lead worship the next Sunday. I decided to spend that week fasting and praying so that God will show up during my ministration, as He did at the festival, and silence the enemy resisting my ministry.

By our next rehearsal, I just knew that God was going to show up because I had so much peace about that Sunday. As faithful as God is, my ministration that Sunday was powerful, to say the least. The presence of God was so strong that something like a mist filled the auditorium during praise and worship. People were so engaged in worship that at a point, almost everyone was on their knees. After a while, I stopped singing and allowed the people to bask in the presence of God. I had not seen such a visitation in a long time. When the pastor took the microphone after the ministration, all she said was, Wow! Wow! What a Presence! After the service, the pastor could not go near us; I could sense that the pastor was embarrassed, and the pastor never made any comment about my ministration again until my family relocated.

God used the situation to draw me closer to Himself so that I can wait on Him to bless His people and silence the devil's resistance to my ministry.

3. How to gain Sensitivity to the Voice of God

The best way music ministers can develop their sensitivity to the spirit of God is to have a relationship with Him. That is by spending a lot of time just waiting on Him (Act. 13:2-3). Jude in his epistle to the Christian Community of his day wrote: *"But you, beloved, build yourselves up [founded] on your most holy faith [make progress, rise like an edifice higher and higher], praying in the Holy Spirit"* (Jud. 1:20 AMP). As we spend time with God; thanking and praising Him, submitting to His will, and obeying His precepts, it will make us more receptive to the voice of God. We must be prepared to spend an hour or more in prayer and praise if we want to recognize the voice of God. I have found that it takes no less than 2 hours to break out of the distractions around us into the heavenly realm, especially when you are just learning to get intimate with the Holy Spirit.

We should remember that we can neither force God to speak to us, earn an answer from Him, nor make ourselves worthy enough to have Him speak to us. Spending a lot of time praying, praising, and obeying biblical principles will make us more open to the leading of the Holy Spirit. It is God's prerogative to speak to us whenever and however He wants, not necessarily when we are praying or praising Him. We are, however, more receptive to His voice when we are in those moments.

Prayer

Dear Father, please teach me to easily recognize your voice always, in Jesus' name I pray, amen!

In the next chapter, I have provided some basic tips to help you develop and maintain your voice.

Chapter 11

Developing and Preserving your Voice

The voice of the vocalist is his/her greatest asset, as the fingers of an organist or a guitarist. Without the voice, the minister will not fulfill their ministry. Very few people are born with good voices, however, the majority of ministers need to undergo specific vocal training to improve their voices. It takes a great deal of time, effort, and discipline to get their voices to the required standard. Interestingly, God has given every vocalist different vocal ranges, keys, and pitches to embellish their ministry and the ability to improve upon their voices. Every minister, therefore, needs to know what they have and work at improving it. This chapter looks at ways to develop and maintain a good singing voice.

1. The Mechanism Behind Voice Production

The mechanism behind the production of musical sounds is complex and very delicate. Every musician needs to understand this mechanism to use their voice effectively and preserve it for a life-long ministry. Primarily, sound production is influenced by the air we allow to flow through our respiratory system, i.e., how we employ the thousands of muscles lined up from our lungs to our lips. Our ability to sing is dependent on the flow of air through the vocal folds and out past the lips.

These folds are placed horizontally behind the middle point of the thyroid cartilage commonly called Adam's Apple. Above the vocal folds is the second fold of tissue called the false vocal folds, which prevent food or water from entering the trachea when swallowing. Above the vocal fold and the false vocal ford is a floppy cartilaginous tongue-shaped structure known as the epiglottis. The epiglottis folds over the opening into the larynx when we swallow and helps prevent materials from getting into the lungs.[114]

The vocal folds are the trachea, or windpipe, which leads to the lungs. This is the most important muscle used in singing. The vocal folds change their positions during singing depending on the type of sounds being made. The sound produced is also influenced by the size of the oral cavity, the position of the lips, the shape, tone, and the position of the tongue. One group of sounds produced is called "*voiced sounds*." They are known as voiced sounds for the reason that their production relies on the vibration of the vocal folds. The other group of sounds is called "*voiceless sounds*." The vocal folds are rarely used in the production of these sounds; rather the sound is produced by turbulent air that flows in parts of the mouth and throat. Examples of voiceless sounds are the early parts of the "*f and the s*" sounds.

---

[114] (MacGibbon 1948)

When singing, the vocal folds are brought together (closed) by the muscles of the larynx. The respiratory muscles and the chest wall cause the air pressure to increase below the vocal folds. When the pressure beneath the vocal folds exceeds the pressure holding them together, the air bursts out and escapes through the folds creating the desired sound. As the air rapidly flows through the larynx, the pressure decreases, and the vocal folds come together again. The pressure beneath the folds rises again, and the process repeats itself. The process of rapid opening and closing produces vocal fold vibration, which together with the movements of the tongue, lips, and other muscles enables the minister to sing so well. Every time the vocal folds open, they produce a jet of air that creates rapid changes in air pressure to produce the musical sounds.[115]

2. Tips For Voice Care

Screaming is one of the bad singing practices that can cause permanent damage to a minister's voice. Screaming can result in what is known as *"singers nodes"*.[116] This is the rapture of the fine fibers of the vocal folds at their ends. MacGibbon describes it as *"the unnatural stretching of the folds and the extra blast of air that can end in damage of the folds."*[117] One can develop a powerful voice with the correct vocal exercises without having to scream. Every voice has its limit; hence every minister must know how far he/she can go in sound production. It has been discovered that our vocal folds collide with each other more

---

[115] (MacGibbon 1948)

[116] (MacGibbon 1948)

[117] Ibid

than a million times during the day when we produce sound, any extra harsh activities such as screaming, put further strain on the already overused vocal folds. A vocalist who wishes to reach a higher pitch can use the peculiar phenomenon known as "*falsetto*." Falsetto is produced by the partial dampening of the false folds when it is forced down on the upper surface of the vocal folds, obliterating the space between the two folds.

Your throat should always be hydrated to stay healthy and lubricated. Drink plenty of fluids every day to keep it hydrated. Due to the delicate nature of the vocal folds, the more hydrated they are, the lesser the strain singing places on the folds. It's however advisable to avoid drinks containing caffeine, alcohol, and other substance that can dehydrate you.

Harsh environments such as smoky, dusty, and noisy environments can affect your voice. Do not take up smoking and if you are already a smoker, quit smoking before this habit destroys your voice. There are thousands of irritants and chemicals in cigarettes that can damage your voice and will certainly shorten your singing career and even your life.

Whenever you develop an infection such as a sore throat, avoid talking for long hours or singing over the problem. This can lead to slower recovery or even small permanent damages to your vocal fold. When you catch a cold do not talk too much. Incorrect voice use, misuse, abuse, or organic or functional problems may result in vocal fatigue. Avoid very cold drinks, junk foods, lots of chocolates, and salty foods. Talking too much when you are scheduled to perform is not very advisable. This may injure your vocal folds.

Eating late, which is less than three hours of bedtime can be injurious to your voice. Acids secreted by your stomach during digestion may end up in your larynx when you lie down to sleep causing a hoarse voice and over the long term, permanent voice damage. Regular heartburn or other symptoms of stomach acid reflux can affect the voice as well as causing other health problems.

3. Warming Up

Although singing appears heavenly, the process is a physical experience. It requires athletic as well as artistry discipline. According to Schoonmaker *"The discipline of singing requires hours of commitment daily: breathing exercises, physical exercises, vocalizing, learning music, practicing, and practicing performing."*[118] Like any athlete, an effective warm-up is essential for optimal performance.

Warming up before any performance is a very powerful way of enabling your vocal folds to perform at their peak. Our vocal folds contain muscles and therefore like any muscle, they need a thorough warm-up before subjecting them to strenuous activity. This will enable your voice to perform at its peak when singing. When this is not done our voices will damage gradually. Vocalization for an hour before your performance can be very helpful.

Warming up allows the singer to connect with her or himself, both physically and spiritually, which is the foundation of a secure vocal technique. Ideally, warming up should not be carried out hurriedly. Adequate time should be allocated for gradual loosening and coordination of the muscles which contribute to vocal production. Warming up should be made

---

[118] (Schoonmaker 2021)

an enjoyable experience. Rushing through it results in physical, as well as, mental tension, thus becoming counter-productive. Ideally, a period of between 10 to 15 minutes is appropriate for a normal warm-up session.

It is expedient to begin by warming up the entire body with gentle physical stretching. This helps ease muscular tension that interferes with vocal production, as well as, stimulates deep breathing, which is necessary for good support of the voice. The muscles of articulation (the jaw, tongue, lips, and soft palate) can be loosened with appropriate exercises, which also can help activate the singer's expiratory airflow. Thankfully, there are a lot of warmup videos online, and a search will help you find an exercise you like. Warming up also relaxes the singer and gives him/her a feeling of wellbeing if he/she is fatigued. It is prudent to start warming up in the most comfortable mid-range of the voice, and gradually work out to the higher and lower extremes of pitch.

It is always advisable to warm down your voice after every ministration with exercises that soothe the vocal folds, for example. "*oo!*") If the singer has been using a "*belting*" voice, it is especially helpful to sing in the "*head*" register (or falsetto), which stretches the vocal folds and alleviates laryngeal tension caused by the "*heavy adjustment.*" Massaging the jaw muscles and other muscles of the neck and shoulders, particularly the trapezius, which arises from the back of the head and vertebrae in the neck and chest, and extends to the collarbones and shoulder blades, provides welcome relief to the singer.

Always keep your arms slightly away from your body. Clasp your hands out in front of you or bring your arms to your side and a bit forward, raising them about 6 inches in a flexible and relaxed manner. This will allow your ribcage to fully expand and your lungs to fill to enable you to project your voice more strongly and clearly. Your feet should be kept about shoulders' width apart; preferably, one foot should be further in front of the other. Be sure you are well balanced yet relaxed. If you must sing while sitting, make sure both feet are flat on the floor, with 12 inches or so between them, and that you are sitting up straight, but not stiffly.

Be relaxed because tension destroys vocal tone. Do not try to let your shoulders hunch up and keep your neck from tensing. Do not force your chest up and out when you breathe in as it will constrict your airflow. Stay in motion, however slightly. This will relax your body and your tone will sound more natural. Try gently swaying from side to side with the rhythm. When you inhale, push your stomach out. This will allow you to fill your lungs. As you exhale, bring your stomach slowly in, using the muscles of your diaphragm, which is just under your ribcage, to control your tone.

If you have to hit a high note or you hear yourself singing flat (that is, if your notes are a tiny bit too low), raise your arms a little higher and smile slightly. When singing very high notes, try closing your eyes and turning your face up slightly. Conversely, if you start to sing sharp (a tiny bit too high), bring your arms down a little lower and open your mouth slightly wider by dropping your lower jaw. Do not dip your chin towards your neck, as this will cause your airflow to become constricted, which will show up in your voice.

Prayer

Father, help me to apply these tips to enhance my ministry to the glory and praise of the One who died and rose triumphantly from the grave, even Jesus the son of the Most High God, and our soon coming King.

Let us now turn our attention to some tips for caring for your musical instruments in the next chapter.

Chapter 12

Caring for your Musical Instrument

In this chapter, I have provided some basic tips Instrumentalists need to maintain their instruments. They may appear rudimentary, but they are the things needed to prolong the life span of your instrument. I have written on four main instruments; the bass guitar, acoustic guitar, electronic keyboard, and the jazz drum for the reason that these instruments are the basic instruments needed for any worship session.

Taking care of your Guitar (bass and acoustic)

Guitars are manufactured with great care. Different types of wood are carefully handpicked and skillfully molded into a beautiful piece of instrument. This makes it an expensive piece of instrument and the musician needs to take good care of it. According to Newbold, "*a guitar player should maintain his instrument with two things in mind: first, to preserve the beauty that is inherent in a well-crafted guitar that was built from quality woods, and second, to keep the instrument in the best possible playing condition.*"[119] Below are a few tips to help maintain your guitar:

1. Clean and polish the guitar regularly with a clean dry cloth. Furniture polish can be used; otherwise, you can buy any polish sold at guitar shops for that purpose. When you follow a regular cleaning and polishing routine, your guitar will always look good and produce good sound.

2. Dress the frets every time you change the strings. If you are a regular player, a lot of sweat, dirt, and oil from your hands build up on the fretboard. This is not good for the strings and may affect the sound quality. Use a very soft-bristled toothbrush and a little soapy water and make sure to wipe the fret dry after cleaning.

3. Wipe down the neck with a dry cloth after every use to protect your fretboard and prolong string life. You will also prolong string life by removing all elements that can cause your strings to deteriorate.

4. Do not expose your instrument to extreme weather conditions for prolonged periods. Heat and sunlight can affect the finishing and make the finely crafted woods of the guitar look old and faded almost overnight. Cold weather may affect the guitar by damaging the binding, inlays, and neck. Guitars need to be kept in a cool, dry environment and away from high humidity. You can

---

[119] (Newbold 2001)

buy a capsule from your guitar store and put it in your case to provide the needed protection.

5. Regularly check and tighten all screws, strap-pins, and tuning machines. This will help avoid any unneeded rattling or jingling when playing your instrument, either at a service or at home for your pleasure.

6. Avoid bringing beverages, drinks, or any liquid near your guitar to avoid any spillage that may cause irreparable damage.

7. Do not allow a child to play with your instrument without an adult's supervision as they may, dis-tune, damage a component or break a string.

8. Avoid scratches or scars on your instrument. Never leave your guitar propped up against the wall or an amplifier because it may fall and break. Buy a stand for your guitar.

9. Ensure that your instrument is properly tuned before playing. There is no better way to keep your guitar in tip-top shape than to play it every day. Remember that as a minister, you need to praise the Lord skillfully, and the more you practice the skillful you become. Play your guitar, take care of it, and you will enjoy it.

Taking care of your Keyboard Instruments

The keyboard instrument, which includes pianos, organs, harpsichords, clavichords, and many others is another important group of instruments in any music band. Below are a few guidelines for maintaining your keyboard instrument from the Canadian Conservation Institute:[120]

1. Regular dusting and wax polishing your keyboard instrument twice a year are appropriate. Light damp cleaning with a slightly moist clean cloth is also effective if the body is in good condition. The keyboard facings of most pianos and other instruments are either ivory or a synthetic substitute. Clean with a soft cloth or swab lightly dampened with water with a few drops of detergent. The keys should not become too wet because ivory keyboards occasionally react to water. It is not advisable to try bleaching piano keys, although bleach may be effective in making them whiter.

2. Open or remove components only with the help of a specialist. Interiors must be dusted very carefully because degraded parts can become loose or detached. Dusting can be done with a soft paintbrush. In places where there are textile components, such as felts or ribbons, a piece of window screening gauze or a piece of clean cloth should be held over the parts being cleaned. This will prevent loose pieces from being sucked away.

3. As soon as a fault is detected, it should be sent for repairs; otherwise, the instrument will be greatly damaged by incautious use, especially where components have been in a derelict or unused condition for long periods.

---

[120] (Canadian Conservation Institute 1999)

4. The keyboard instruments should be moved with care because of their many detachable or loose parts. Tuning and maintaining your keyboard instruments should be done by specialists.

5. Do not put any heavy objects on the keyboard as that may cause considerable damage to the instrument. When playing, keep all cables neatly arranged and away from the walkways to prevent someone from mistakenly pulling the instrument to the ground. Always raise your volume moderately to avoid damaging your speakers with the loud volume.

Taking Care of Your Percussion Instruments (Drum Set)

The Jazz drum is part of the group of instruments called percussion instruments and they are pretty sturdy. Taking care of your drums, cymbals, hardware, and other drum accessories comes down to common sense. If you handle your equipment right, it should last you a lifetime. Buying new gear should only be the result of a desire to upgrade, not the result of poor instrument management.[121] Below are a few tips for maintaining your drum set by Starr:

1. Regularly cleaning and polishing your instrument should become your habit. This will keep your drums in good working condition all the time.

---

[121] (Starr 2007)

215

2. Care should be taken when transporting your drums. When you have to move your instruments, disassemble them, and store the components of your drums set in separate cases to avoid scratches or damage. Moving the components around may be perilous for your bottom snare drumhead. It is advisable to label the drum cases differently for easy identification to avoid lifting and dropping, opening, and closing every case when looking for a component.

Incorrectly storing bass drum pedals and hi-hat stands in hardware bags can cause the footboard stabilizer rod on the bass drum pedal and/or the foot pedal linkage rod on the hi-hat pedal to crack. It is good to put your bass drum pedal on top of all the other stands in your hardware bag or case. This will protect it from getting crushed by heavier, double-braced cymbal and snare stands.

Avoid carrying your bass drum in a case over your shoulder as it may drop, and the hoop may crack. Consider transporting the bass drum in a hard plastic case, even though this will make the drum bulky. Bass drums are particularly vulnerable because of the wooden hoop fittings, which make them large and heavy. This head is ultra-thin, and a bass drum spike or cymbal stand can easily pierce through the mylar, rendering the drum useless.

3. Do not expose your drums to extreme weather conditions as they may damage your instrument. Leaving the drums in an extremely hot or cold condition, especially in a vehicle, could cause plastic veneers on your drums to peel off and/or crack. Do not leave your instrument

lying unattended to or allow children to play with the drums set without any adult's supervision as they may be run over or broken.

4. Setting up your drums can promote or prevent damage to your equipment. One common mistake is placing your snare drum too close to your 12-inch rack tom-tom. Since it hovers over the snare drum at a slightly higher level, the rim of the snare drum can rub against the tom-tom as you play. Heavy playing will cause your whole drum kit to shake, if your snare drum is touching the tom-tom, it will scrape the varnish and even cut into the wood of the drum itself. Always watch when playing and back up your snare drum immediately you see this occurring.

It is advisable to raise your cymbals high enough to enable you to strike them on the edge multiple times when you are playing extremely loud music. This will help you produce a nice, clean hit even as the cymbal bobs downward. It will also help you play the cymbals loudly with articulated crashes without the cymbal tackling with under the weight.

For general cymbal health, keep the wing nut loose on top of the cymbal, use a washer and felt pad under the cymbal, and make sure you place a nylon or rubber sleeve on the threaded portion of the cymbal arm; this is the very tip of the cymbal stand that touches the cymbal itself. If you do not use a sleeve, the cymbal will not only rattle on the stand, but it will also become, as drummers call it, "*key-holed*." This means that the center hole of the cymbal will wear down and resemble an old-fashioned keyhole on a door.

5. Using an appropriate stick will affect your cymbal longevity. Only wooden drumsticks should be used to play, as they help to take the burden off of each crash. After multiple uses, wooden sticks begin to break down and chip. This is actually good! You want to use a durable stick; however, care should be taken when striking the cymbal as heavy strokes can cause it to fall on the snare drums. Choose the appropriate stick to help you produce a good sound. Cracking a cymbal or two is unavoidable in the ministry of a drummer. However, it should not be a frequent occurrence.

6. When tuning your drum set, do not fasten the wing nut on your cymbal tilter or the tuning pegs on the drums down too tightly. This will limit the cymbal's ability to waver and dip as you strike it, thus choking the sound of the cymbal and interfering with the cymbal's ability to endure the impact of the stick. If not checked, it can crack your cymbal. Do not fasten the knobs of the Mylar tightly, as it can lead to a tear.

In conclusion, caring for your instrument should be a habit. Remember, without it, you cannot fulfill your calling as an instrumentalist. Also remember your need to practice, practice and practice. Make it a habit to practice at least one hour every day to build your confidence and play skillfully to the glory and honor of our King.

Prayer

God richly bless you as you put the content of this book into practice.

AMEN!!!

Appendix

Abbreviations

ASV	American Standard Version
AMP	Amplify Bible
BBE	Basic Bible English
ESV	English Standard Version
HCSB	Holman Christian Standard Bible
ISBE	International Standard Bible Encyclopedia
NCV	New Century Version
NIV	New International Version
NLT	New Living Translation
MKJV	Modern King James Version
NKJV	New King James Version

Bibliography

Barnes, Albert. 1845. "Albert Barnes' Notes on the Whole
Bible: Isaiah 14:12." Truth According to Scripture. 1845.
https://www.truthaccordingtoscripture.com/commen-
taries/bnb/isaiah-14.php#.YblcPnzMLcs.

Batterson, Mark. 2017. *Whisper: How to Hear the Voice of
God*. USA: Multnomah.

Baxter, Mary K. 2003. *A Divine Revelation of Angels*.
Nevada, USA: Whitaker House.

Boschman, LaMar. 1980. *The Rebirth of Music*.
Shippensburg, PA: Destiny Image Publishers Inc.

Boshart, David. 2006. "Symbolism in the Bible–Christ-
Centered Mall Teaching." 2006. https://christcentered-
mall.com/teachings/symbolism/index.htm.

Brickner, David. 2006. *Christ in the Feast of Tabernacles*.
Chicago: Moody Publishers. https://www.scribd.com/
book/314659665/Christ-in-the-Feast-of-Tabernacles.

Brown, Francis, S. R. Driver, and Charles A. Briggs. 1976.
The Brown-Driver-Briggs' Hebrew and English Lexicon.
USA: Moody Publishers.

Canadian Conservation Institute. 1999. "How to Care for
Keyboard Instrument." 1999. http://www.cciicc.gc.ca/car-
ingfor-prendresoindes/articles/434-eng.aspx.

Cheong, W. 1999. "How to Prepare for Worship." 1999.
http://www.worshipworld.com/tips.htm.

Erb, Clayton. 2009. "Seminar Session 2–Psalms, Hymns, and
Spiritual Songs." 2009. https://www.gracechurch.org/
sermons/topics/74?show=all.

Fitzpatrick, G. 1984. *How to Recognize God's Voice*. USA:
Spiritual Growth Books.

GARDEN CITY. 2021. "A Musical Devotion
On Praise." 2021. https://www.bible.com/
reading-plans/4496-a-musical-devotion-on-praise.

Gill, John. 1809. *John Gill's Exposition of the Entire Bible*.
Public Domain.

Godtube. 2021. "It Is Well With My Soul–Lyrics, Hymn
Meaning and Story." GodTube. 2021. https://www.god-
tube.com/popular-hymns/it-is-well-with-my-soul/.

Hammond, C. 2013. "When It Comes to Conversation,
Are Women Really More Likely to Be Bigger
Talkers than Men?" 2013. www.bbc.com/future/
article/20131112-do-women-talk-more-than-men.

Hayford, J. E, and G Matsdorf. 1991. *Commentary on Paul's
Epistle to the Ephesians*. 1991st ed. USA: Nashville:
Spirit-Filled Life Bible.

Hughes, James R. 2006. "In Spirit and Truth: Worship as God Requires (Understanding and Applying the Regulative Principle of Worship)," 160.

James, Orr, John Nuelsen, Edgar Mullins, Morris Evans, and Melvin Grove Kyle, eds. 1939. "Music." In *International Standard Bible Encyclopedia*. Vol. Five volume set. Wm. B. Eerdmans Publishing Co.

Johnson, B. W. 2017. *The People's New Testament: The Common and Revised Version with References*. Public Domain: Cross Reach Publication. http://www.thebible. net/reference/pnt/PNT00.HTM.

Kwapong, Eric. 2001. *True Worship Experience: Entering into the Presence of God*. USA: Beacon of Glory International.

Leonard, R. 1993. "Biblical Philosophy of the Worship Arts." In *The Complete Library of Christian Worship*, edited by R. E Webber, 1:221–22. Peabody-Massachusetts, USA: Hendrickson Publishers.

MacArthur, John. n.d. "In Music Worship?" Mp3. Music. Accessed December 14, 2021. https://www.gracechurch. org/sermons/topics/74?show=all.

MacGibbon, T. A. 1948. "The Mechanism of Voice Production." 49 1948. http://rsnz.natlib.govt.nz/volume/ rsnz_77.html.

McCasland, David C. 2014. "Wait on the Lord." Daily Devotional. March 2, 2014. https://dailydevotionalz. wordpress.com/tag/david-c-mccasland/.

McCracken, Andy. 1978. *A Modern English Translation of the Ethiopian Book of Enoch with Introduction and Notes By*. Edited by Michael A. Knibb. UK: University of London.

McGawan, H. B. 1997. *The Tabernacle: God's Complete Plan of Salvation to All Mankind*. Revised edition. Canada: Toronto: World Christian Ministries.

Merriam-Webster. 2011. *Webster's American English Dictionary*. Newest Edition. Springfield, Massachusetts: Merriam-Webster Inc.

Murdock, M. 1999. *The Young Minister's Handbook*. USA: Murdock Association.

Murray, Andrew. 1998. *Andrew Murray on Prayer*. USA: Whitaker House.

Newbold, B. 2001. "Caring for Your Guitar." 2001. http://www.cs.utah.edu/~bnewbold/guitarguide/care.html.

Phiri, Alex. 2008. "Ambition for Position." Presented at the Church Service, On Eagles' Wing Church, IK, November 17.

Pobee, L. 2009. *Thanksgiving and Praise: Believers' Assurance of Sustained Inflow of Divine Power*. Accra, Ghana: The Praise Revolution.

Puls, Ken. 2007. "Music and the Church: Finding Our Voice in Worship." *Founders Journal*, no. 67: 5.

Rea, Ed. 2021. "Whatever Your Hand Finds to Do, Do It with Your Might; for There Is No Work or Device or

Knowledge or Wisdom in the Grave Where You Are Going." *Pastor Ed's Devotional* (blog). 2021. http://packinghouseredlands.org/devotional/?p=8775.

Schoonmaker, Bruce. 2021. "The Tao of Singing." 2021. http://facweb.furman.edu/~bschoonmaker/sing.html.

Smith, William. 2016. "Gospels." Public Domain. Biblestudytools.Com. 2016. https://www.biblestudytools. com/dictionaries/smiths-bible-dictionary/gospels.html.

Spurgeon, Charles H. 1885. "The Treasury of David (Abridged)." 1885. https://archive.org/details/ treasury_david_vol1_1104_librivox.

Starr, E. 2007. "Taking Care of Drums, Cymbals, and Other Equipment on Gigs." 2007. http://www.upublish.info/ Article/Taking-Care-Of-Drums—Cymbals—And-Other-Equipment-On-Gigs-/107280.

Strong, James. 2009. *Strong's Exhaustive Concordance*. Hendrickson Publishers. https://www.christianbook.com/strongs-exhaustive-concordance-updated-edition-kjv/9781598563788/ pd/563788.

Thayer, Joseph. 2017. *Thayer's Greek-English Lexicon of the New Testament: Coded With the Numbering System from Strong's Exhaustive Concordance of the Bible*. Stanford Inversiones SpA.

Tozer, A.W. 2006. *Whatever Happened to Worship?: A Call to Worship*. USA: Moody Publishers. https://www.thriftbooks.com/w/

whatever-happened-to-worship-a-call-to-true-worship_
aw-tozer/300187/.

Tracy, Linda. 2005. "Biblical Worship Is Good for You."
2005. http://www.laudemount.org/a-bwigfy.htm#fn11.

Tuttle, C. 1989. "Foundations of Praise and Worship." In
*In Spirit and Truth: Exploring Directions in Music in
Worship Today*, edited by R Sheldon. London: Hodder &
Stoughton.

Warren, Rick. 2002. *The Purpose-Driven Life*. USA:
Zondervan.

CPSIA information can be obtained
at www.ICGtesting.com
Printed in the USA
LVHW051359090322
712905LV00013B/940

9 781662 842047